DOUBLE WEBS

Light on the Secret Agents' War in France

Jean Overton Fuller

DOUBLE WEBS

Published by Sapere Books.

24 Trafalgar Road, Ilkley, LS29 8HH

United Kingdom

saperebooks.com

ISBN: 978-1-80055-751-2.

TABLE OF CONTENTS

FOREWORD

by
Dame Irene Ward, D.B.E., M.P.

This is an objective and independent book which is complementary to Miss Jean Overton Fuller's previous publications. The integrity of her research is clear to see.

Miss Overton Fuller's readers will remember that in her moving and factual book *Madeleine* she endeavoured to give the fullest account of her friend Noor Inayat Khan's secret war work, and her contacts in France in pursuit of knowledge revealed many curious incidents on which official comment has been silent.

There will always be those who deprecate any 'raking of the ashes' but I feel we owe an equal debt of gratitude to those who served and did not survive as to those who triumphantly returned. Their names also deserve to be recorded faithfully in contemporary history.

For the future, too, some of the disadvantages as well as the advantages of creating an organisation such as S.O.E. using both official and amateur secret service agents together may be worth considering. The facts so cogently presented in this book have far-reaching implications.

Miss Overton Fuller has wisely attempted no analysis or surmise but allows the facts to stimulate the mind.

There has been no official history of Special Operations Executive but, in the interests of those who served in it, I hope Miss Overton Fuller's remarkable though in places disconcerting story will be widely studied.

A man's a man, for a' that
ROBERT BURNS

CHAPTER ONE: THE QUESTION OF THE MAIL

Publication of *The Starr Affair* left me free to give my mind to "Gilbert" and with "Gilbert" was associated the question of the mail. In *The Starr Affair* I had considered the question of the radio sets.

I had learned about these whilst engaged on research for my first book, *Madeleine*. But *Madeleine* had been the biography of an individual, Noor Inayat Khan to give her her real name, who had been my friend in private life; when I, who had never belonged to the Special Operations Executive (S.O.E.), began my enquiries on the Continent, it had been solely with the intention of writing her personal story, and so I avoided operational questions where they did not bear on it. Until the publication in 1949 of the Official Citation for the posthumous award to her of the George Cross, I had never even heard of S.O.E., or its "French Section"[1] in which she served. She had spent at my flat her last night of leave in London, and with the passage of time I had come to believe she must have gone back to France, where she had been brought up, in order to work with the Resistance; but it was only from the citation that I learned she had in fact been landed in France by Lysander aircraft on June 16th, 1943, and worked as a radio operator under the code-name of "Madeleine" until betrayed to the Germans.

---

[1] Note that "French Section" was the name of the British directed section of S.O.E. concerned with France; it was *not* the section run by the French.

My researches had begun from the moment I read this and had taken me to France and Germany. From the people whom I had interviewed in those countries, I had learned that after her capture on October 13th, 1943, her radio-set had been played back by the Germans to London (a process which became known as the 'radio-game'), and that London had, until the following spring, accepted the messages as genuine. But she had never known about this, and in that sense it was no part of her personal story.

"Madeleine's" radio had not, however, been the only one to be played back in this manner. Captain John Starr who had likewise been a prisoner at 84 Avenue Foch, H.Q. of the *Sicherheitsdienst*, had realised that further men and women were being sent over from London in response to the fatal messages sent over several radio circuits to drop straight into German hands as they came down; and it was the course of action which he had taken in consequence of his knowledge that constituted the whole interest of his story. I had gone to see him in the first place solely to ask his witness concerning "Madeleine"; but he had told me not only what he knew of her but the whole of his own story, and after *Madeleine* I had written *The Starr Affair*. In that, all the operational interest had turned around radio sets.

But even while I was writing that, I had realised that the radio sets were not the whole of the question. "Madeleine" had been sent out to join the "Prosper" network, arriving a few days before the disaster that overtook it. She had been intended to act as assistant radio operator to "Archambault," "Prosper's" first radio operator and second in command, though she was left without a chief by the catastrophe which fell just after her arrival. On June 24th, 1943, the two

Englishmen, "Prosper" and "Archambault," together with their French girl courier, "Denise," were arrested.

The "Prosper" network, which covered Paris itself and extended down the whole of the Loire valley, was the most important of the "French Section" networks in France; it was a kind of master-network to which a number of others, pre-existing and partly indigenous, including surviving elements from some of those weakened in earlier waves of arrests, had allowed themselves to become, in varying degrees, tributary.[2]

S.O.E. was an organisation concerned not with intelligence but with sabotage; its principal function was the equipment and organisation of a secret army intended to rise when the Invasion was mounted; a major part of its work consisted therefore in the reception and storage of arms sent from London and dropped by parachute at every moon. S.S. Sturmbannführer Kieffer, commandant of the *Sicherheitsdienst* at 84 Avenue Foch, now offered "Prosper" a pact, by the terms of which the lives and good treatment of all those who had operated under his direction were guaranteed in return for disclosure of the places where the arms were stored. "Prosper" accepted the pact; and "Archambault" was made responsible for explaining it to the organisers of subsidiary sectors as they were brought in, in order that it might be carried through.

In every case that had come to my knowledge, these had likewise fallen in with the terms of the pact. The arms had been stored, necessarily, in numerous small piles on the private premises of consenting householders. Disclosing the addresses was, therefore, a delicate matter; but, whilst the arrests in the "Prosper" network spread within two or three weeks to

---

[2] Lt.-Col. Buckmaster writes in *Specially Employed* that the "Prosper" network comprised some 10,000 people, though this is probably a loose figure.

something like 500, it was impossible to say that all these derived from the pact.

Kieffer honoured his side of the bargain for so long as the prisoners remained in his control. But when, in 1944, Kieffer's service had to prepare its withdrawal from Paris, the prisoners were sent ahead to Germany; and in Germany the pact was lost sight of. Some of those whom it should have protected met their deaths in the concentration camps and these included "Prosper" and "Archambault" themselves, and "Denise" and "Madeleine" (though "Madeleine", having been arrested so long afterwards, might not have been considered as under its protection).

The French members of the "Prosper" network who survived to return and explain to their own authorities, after the war, their concordance in the pact, had been exonerated. Nevertheless, the pact had become the subject of a great deal of discussion in France. Those who had served under "Prosper" held him in the very highest regard and felt sure his only consideration had been to save his men; indeed, it could very well be argued that had he refused his ear to Kieffer's proposal, he would have thrown away a possible chance of saving their lives. As plain clothes agents, neither he nor those who had accepted his orders could claim protection as Prisoners of War. The clauses in the Hague Convention, defining categories of persons to be and not to be considered as spies, made no provision for such as these; if they were sent for trial, it would be likely to be held that they were spies and the death penalty would follow. At the very best, their position was anomalous; but by agreeing to enter into a pact, "Prosper" did obtain for them a certain status, the status of persons protected by the pact. Some felt, however, that a German guarantee should not have been accepted.

But the pact and all that followed from the arrest of "Prosper" and "Archambault" was surely the consequence of some prior leak. The big mystery was how "Prosper" and "Archambault" themselves had come to be arrested.

A German, Ernest, had told me it was through the mail. Ernest was not a regular member of the *Sicherheitsdienst*. He had settled in France as a young man and was during the early part of the war interned by the French. When the Germans occupied the country he had been released and attached to Kieffer's service in the first place solely as personal interpreter to Kieffer himself in his daily business. Later, when the Resistance grew serious and prisoners were brought in, he had found himself interpreting between Kieffer and the prisoners. Kieffer was sufficiently perceptive to realise that Ernest's mild and unprofessional manner disarmed the prisoners and won their confidence and he made the experiment of letting him question one on his own. He was pleased with the result and let him continue.

After this, Ernest interrogated all the major agents of the British (S.O.E.) "French Section".

Of the prisoners who passed through his hands, none had made any complaint against him, and more than one had told me personally they had found him 'human.' After the war he had been examined and released, and at the *Tribunal Militaire Permanent de Paris* they gave me the address in Germany he had left them.

I had gone to Germany in 1950 (it was my first visit to that country) to ask Ernest what he could tell me of "Madeleine." He had been most helpful and co-operative, and during a series of meetings our conversations had ranged over a large number of subjects. Though I did not need it for *Madeleine*, I had asked him how "Prosper" and "Archambault" came to be arrested.

It was through the mail, he said. Both of them used to send back to London long handwritten reports; these were brought to the German H.Q. on the Avenue Foch where they were photostatted before being returned in order that they might be forwarded by aircraft to London. They contained very comprehensive information concerning the operations of the network in the field including the addresses used as post-boxes, and it was, he supposed, this information which enabled Kieffer's service to arrest the principals when they considered the moment as ripe. (The reports were in plain language, not encoded.)

At a later date, "Madeleine" had also sent a long handwritten report to London (radio messages had to be couched in telegraphic language and kept short) which was similarly photostatted, as was a personal letter she had written to her mother. He still remembered the way the envelope was addressed.

This was comparatively early in my investigations; but, though I had no knowledge of secret work when I started, it was evident to me that what I was being told was extraordinary. 'Who brought you the reports?' I asked him.

'Kieffer gave them to me,' was his reply.

I took this to mean he did not know who had given them to Kieffer or to Kieffer's service. I exclaimed that surely a traitor must have been at work; "Prosper" and "Archambault" and afterwards "Madeleine" must have given these reports to somebody whom they believed would loyally ensure their transmission to London, and this person must have passed them to the Germans treacherously. Ernest did not reply.

Starr had not belonged to the "Prosper" network, so he had been right outside this drama. He had been Organiser, of a smaller but quite independent network of the "French Section" in the Dijon area.

When brought to the Avenue Foch he had, like other prisoners, been shown the mass of photostatted copies of the reports sent to London from the "Prosper" network; for the Germans displayed these to show the extent of their penetration of the "French Section." But from his point of view the question of the mail was less important than that of the radio sets.

Whilst I was writing *The Starr Affair*, a very important book appeared. This was *London Calling North Pole*[3] by Lt-Col. H. J. Giskes, former head of German Counter-Espionage in Holland, Belgium and Northern France. In it, Col. Giskes revealed that starting from March, 1942, every single one of the radio-circuits of S.O.E. "Dutch Section" had for a period of eighteen months been German controlled, and that all the men and cargoes parachuted into Holland during that period had been received on the landing fields by the Germans. For Starr, as for me, this was the first intimation that the radio-game had been played from elsewhere than France.

Colonel Giskes, who wrote Dutch as well as German, had had his book published in the first instance in Holland, where a Dutch Parliamentary Committee had sat for two years in investigation of "North Pole" as the Germans had called this operation. That Colonel Giskes should have chosen to publish his book in the country most involved, and so very seriously concerned, seemed an earnest that the book must be solid.

When it appeared in England, the English public was unprepared for it. Mr. Eden, in reply to a question from a Labour member, told the House of Commons that the substance of Lt.-Col. Giskes's book was believed to be true.

---

[3] Kimber, 1953.

About this time, while *The Starr Affair* was still in preparation, a friend gave me two German books, both by Erich Borchers and published by Adolf Sponholtz Verlag, Hanover. The first, *La Chatte*, was the story of a French woman who had worked first for the Allies then for the Germans after capture on December 18th, 1941, and whose radio set had for a while been played back from Paris to London under the direction of Borchers.

The second book, *Monsieur Jean*, concerned the further adventures of an N.C.O., Sergeant Bleicher,[4] who had assisted Borchers in tracking down "La Chatte" and the *Interalliée*, and in handling the case. As a matter of fact, this was the book I tackled first for, in turning the pages, I saw the familiar name of Kieffer. I did not, at that time read German; but, convinced that what this book contained might be important, I sat down to it with a German-English dictionary and a grammar. It took me a whole day to make out the sense of the first page. There were 218 pages in the book. I set my teeth and, at my snail's pace, went forward. Speed increased with practice and, though it cost me literally much headache, I reached the end in a couple of months.

There proved to be a good deal about radio sets in this book, too. But there was also something else. There was mention of a man called Gilbert, of whom I had never heard previously and whose nationality I was unable to discover from the text. According to Bleicher's appreciation:[5]

---

[4] The Borchers books concerned with "La Chatte" and Bleicher, published by Sponholtz. should not be confused with other writings by another German author which feature Bleicher as the central character but which I find so much fictionalised as to be useless for serious study.

[5] P. 115.

Gilbert was the most important double-agent of Sturmbannführer Kieffer. He worked for him and for London. He was a quite unscrupulous man and was lacking in that inner sense of right conduct which characterised every other agent I have known, for whichever side he worked. Gilbert was wholly selfish. He worked only for his own profit. For that, he was capable of anything, even treason. He was what soldiers call a swine.

According to the narrative, Bleicher had had dealings with such a number of double-agents and traitors that it struck me as remarkable he should pick one from the rest for this moral appraisal. But Gilbert, it appeared, had been getting in the way of Roger, and therein lay Bleicher's concern. Roger Bardet was a Frenchman who, though trusted by Major Frager of the "French Section", informed on Frager and his network over a long period to Bleicher of the *Abwehr*.[6] Between the *Sicherheitsdienst* and the *Abwehr* there existed always a certain rivalry, and this, it appeared, extended to Allied nationals in intelligence with either; in any case it was to Bleicher's interest to see Roger, his own agent, preferred above Gilbert, hence probably the partiality.

A little further on,[7] Bleicher referred to a visit paid to France in the summer of 1943 by Major Nicholas Boddington, second in command to Lt.-Col. Buckmaster, head of the "French Section." Bleicher declared that he had first had intelligence of Major Boddington's visit from Roger, and that a few days afterwards he had had a telephone conversation about it with

---

[6] Frager was hanged at Buchenwald on October 4th, 1944, after having been arrested by Bleicher in consequence of this betrayal.
[7] P. 117.

Kieffer, and had suggested that Kieffer, if he wished to arrest Major Boddington, could surely learn his whereabouts from Gilbert.

'Gilbert must know where he is.'

Kieffer growled, 'Apparently not. Gilbert learned only by accident that Boddington was in Paris. But his arrival can't have been arranged without the knowledge and help of the French Section. I suspect Paul [Major Frager] of having arranged the whole thing.'

Following this conversation, Bleicher surmised:

Gilbert must have had his hand in it. The arrangements for Boddington's visit to Paris must have been made between him and London. Gilbert must also know where Boddington was staying. If he pretended to Kieffer not to know, he must have a special object. It could be one of two things: either he wanted to throw doubt on Roger, for if Paul [Major Frager] had arranged things Roger must have known about it; or he could have another reason: could Boddington stay in Paris without being arrested, it would be [for London] a proof of Gilbert's absolute reliability. Were Boddington to return to London safely it would appear, there, that the warning Paul had given them against Gilbert was groundless.

It was a complicated passage, which I had to read a number of times before I was sure that I had got the sense of it. If Gilbert had in fact known where Boddington was staying and had told Kieffer he did *not* know, that would, in the simplest interpretation, suggest a higher loyalty to London; but

Bleicher's contention was that Gilbert had kept Boddington's address secret from Kieffer not from veritable loyalty to London, but to safeguard his reputation in London and disarm any suspicion concerning his activities which might exist there.

From the end of the book, I learned that Roger Bardet had after the war been tried by the French Justice on a charge of intelligence with the enemy, and convicted;[8] but nothing was said about what had happened to Gilbert. From the text it seemed that he was of Allied nationality, and a member of the "French Section"; I could suppose that "Gilbert" was a code-name, but I had never heard of an agent of the "French Section" who bore that codename.

There was one other passage in this book which interested me; that was the assertion that through the agency of Roger, Bleicher had been put into contact first with a French girl, Denise, and then with an Englishman with whom she worked, a Mr. Ellis; and that Mr. Ellis had handed over to Roger photographs of members of his group in order that Roger might have identity cards made out for them; and that these identity cards had been made out by the *Abwehr* for them and duplicates kept on the *Abwehr* files.

I wondered whether Denise was the "Denise", courier to "Prosper" and "Archambault."

In the spring of 1954, when *The Starr Affair* was already in this press, this book appeared in England, under the title *Colonel Henri's Story* from Kimber, translated, annotated (and somewhat expurgated) by Mr. Ian Colvin. Mr. Colvin definitely identified "Denise" with Miss Andrée Borrel, which I knew by this time to be the real name of "Prospers" courier. Mr. Colvin also appeared, from his notes, to accept the authenticity of the

---

[8] The death sentence was afterwards commuted to one of imprisonment and he has now been set at provisional liberty.

story of the photographs which had been handed over and of the identity cards; but he gave no clue as to the identity of Mr. Ellis. (For a long time, I wondered if "Ellis" were another name for "Prosper", but later a Frenchwoman, Madame Lebras, who served with the "Prosper" network, told me that there was another Englishman in the field who was known as "Ellis" and that "Denise", amongst other things, acted as liaison between "Prosper" and "Ellis").

But what interested me more than anything was that Mr. Colvin had put a note to the passage concerning "Gilbert" and Major Boddington's visit:

> Colonel Buckmaster has identified Gilbert to the Editor as the code-name for his air movements officer in France... Gilbert, a Frenchman, is today at liberty, despite the suspicions that Bleicher tries to cast on him. As for the Boddington mission, it was a distinct success...

Air Movements Officer! Four years ago, Ernest had told me that "Prosper", "Archambault" and their colleagues had been arrested in consequence of the interception of the mail they had sent to London, and that the mail, after it had been photostatted, had been forwarded to London by aircraft. Even then it had appeared to me that only somebody acting as liaison between the principals of the "Prosper" network and the aircraft could have passed it to the Germans before forwarding. I had never known that there was a special man charged by the "French Section" with the duties of Air Movements Officer; now that I knew that there was, and that he was this "Gilbert", he became, for me, a suspect.

The Starr Affair was published on July 26th, 1954. I sent a copy to Ernest, and he wrote back to thank me, saying he thought it very courageous of Starr to tell the full story. 'It is with great pleasure that I have read this account of things as they really happened; that I can certify.'

When I had, four years ago, plied Ernest with questions concerning the interception of the mail, of which he had spoken, he had not been anxious to develop the subject. I had taken silence to mean that he did not know more than he had said. It struck me suddenly that, if this were indeed a very critical and delicate matter, he might then have thought it inadvisable to speak of it in greater detail with somebody he had only just met. Now that the passage of time had allowed him to gain a confidence in me, such as I had in him, it might be different.

I wrote thanking him for his tribute to *The Starr Affair* and asking him whether he had, by any chance, ever met or heard of "Gilbert."

His reply astounded me. 'I know "Gilbert" and his affair very well and I gave evidence about it to the *Tribunal Militaire de Paris* in 1949.' When he did so, "Gilbert", whose real name was known to the British and French authorities, had already been tried and acquitted, and it was therefore impossible to publish anything concerning him. 'It is the most distressing case I have known, much graver than the affair of ———.'[9] I could only tell you about it verbally, not in writing. Know only that I consider him responsible for the great disaster of the "French Section" in 1943 when "Prosper", "Archambault" and their colleagues were arrested.

I replied telling him I would come to Germany again as soon as I was able, though that would not be for a few weeks.

---

[9] Then he named a case in which he had given evidence for the prosecution but which had resulted in an acquittal.

CHAPTER TWO: YEO-THOMAS

A considerable polemic in the press had followed publication of *The Starr Affair*, and I found that I had sympathy in a quarter I had not thought of.

My knowledge of the structure of S.O.E. had grown up piecemeal. It was, for example, only from somebody in the B.B.C. that I learned that the head of S.O.E. for all the countries in Europe and Asia in which it operated was Major-General Sir Colin Gubbins, K.C.M.G. And it was only when *The White Rabbit* appeared that I learned from its pages that there had been two sections operating in France: the British-directed "French Section" under Lt.-Col. Buckmaster, and R.F. (*République Française*) Section which, though British, dealt exclusively with General de Gaulle's B.C.R.A. (*Bureau Central de Renseignements et Action*) commanded by Colonel Dewavrin alias "Passy." Wing-Commander Yeo-Thomas, G.C., M.C., alias "The White Rabbit", had served with R.F.

Yeo-Thomas had become, since the war, head of the Federation of British Industries in Paris and normally lived there; but now I learned from some of his former colleagues in R.F. that he was at the moment in a hospital in England, having come over in order to undergo a major surgical operation. Next, one of these colleagues told me that he had been to the hospital to see Yeo-Thomas, who had now had the operation, and had taken him *The Starr Affair* as being more in his line than the traditional grapes. Yeo-Thomas was interested; he was coming out on September 16th and suggested I should telephone him at his London flat on the evening of that day.

I did so rather timidly for it seemed to me that as he had only come out of hospital that day he might be feeling too weak really to want to consider other people's problems. It was Barbara Yeo-Thomas who answered the phone and said, 'I'll get Tommy.'

'I can't see anything wrong with what Starr did!' were, I think, the first words Yeo-Thomas spoke to me over the phone.[10] Whilst himself a prisoner at the Avenue Foch he had seen Starr more than once, and that during the period which was in question. He gave me in a few words his own very cogent digest of the situation, and asked me to meet him for a drink on the next day but one, Saturday, September 18th, at his favourite Bloomsbury pub, *The Friend at Hand*.

I arrived too early and awaited, in a strange and almost nervous state of expectancy the arrival of this man who had been one of the great heroic figures of the French Resistance and who had suffered appalling experiences after his capture. And then he came in: short, tough, incredibly tough; but I realised in a very few minutes there was more than toughness; there was sensibility.

He got pink gins for both of us, and plunged straight into the subject of Starr, filling in with greater detail the appreciation of the situation at the Avenue Foch which he had given me over the telephone. 'If there's an Enquiry, I'll give evidence for Starr,' he said. 'You can tell Starr that.'

The picture of Avenue Foch I had given in *Madeleine* and *The Starr Affair*, based on the evidence given me by "French Section" agents who had been there as prisoners, perplexed

---

[10] *The Starr Affair* dealt at length with the suggestion made by some of those responsible in London that Starr had whilst a prisoner gone amiss in manoeuvering for a position of greater freedom, even though the object of this was to find a means of alerting London to the radio-game.

some readers by an unexpected mildness and almost complete absence of reference to real brutality. I knew this must be in Yeo-Thomas's mind when he said:

'By the way, people *were* beaten up at the Avenue Foch, because I was.' He said this quietly, but as he said it he looked me very deep in the eyes and I knew that he was a man telling the truth.

I had studied *The White Rabbit* intensively. When first I read it my reaction had made me physically ill for two or three days. Since then, I had been over the Avenue Foch passages so often that I almost knew them by heart. But I thought I knew the answer; the R.F. prisoners had been handled in a different department from those of the "French Section." I put this to him, saying that my books treated only the department in which the "French Section" agents were handled and that none of their men seemed to have been treated anything like he was.

'I know that,' he said. I was very relieved. He had travelled from Paris to Buchenwald in a carriage with twenty-eight agents of the "French Section", and they had told him they had not been beaten up whilst at the Avenue Foch. 'I was *very surprised*, because *I had been*.' His choice of words was simple; it was only the emphasis and intonation which gave them terrific point. He thought he must have been beaten on every occasion that he was brought to the Avenue Foch (not to speak of elsewhere in the meantime). 'But some of them had been there for weeks and yet they told me they had not been beaten up.' He had been at a loss to understand it, until it flashed upon him that they were all "French Section" men and that he was the only one from R.F. in the party. He believed that most of his colleagues in R.F. had suffered the same treatment as himself.

We went into the question of the interrogators; excepting that he had been seen at one moment by Dr. Goetz (who had been 'correct'), they all seemed to be different. 'Your Ernest is *not* my Ernst Mizzlewitz, is he?' he asked me. I told him the surname of 'my' Ernest. He said he had realised, while he was there, that there were two of them; the name of 'his' had been pronounced in the German way with only one 'E', but he caught references to another whose name was pronounced as in French with a second 'e' inserted. 'I believe I glimpsed your Ernest for about thirty seconds. Or perhaps a minute. Not longer.'

I was wrestling with the problem of how two such very different worlds had existed, sealed off from each other to the extent which apparently they were, within such narrow confines. My Ernest, to whom I had sent a copy of *The White Rabbit*, was convinced, I told him, that in as much as he belonged not to the "French Section" but to R.F., his interrogation must have taken place not in 84 but in 86, where, Ernest believed, all the de Gaulle people were handled.

A lesser man might have taken offence. Yeo-Thomas did not. He thought it was 84 but was perfectly willing to go into it, to see whether there was the possibility that he could have made a mistake. He had certainly spent a day and a half in a cell in 84; one of the bars of the skylight bore obvious traces of having been removed and then replaced more securely. He was told that this was the cell from which Starr had succeeded in climbing out; and indeed it was plain that 'the whole job had been strengthened to prevent any future escape.' That it was Starr's ex-cell, confirmed that it was in 84. On the other hand, he had, to the best of his knowledge, never seen Sturmbannführer Kieffer, the commandant of 84, and, seeing that Kieffer interviewed even the most minor of the prisoners brought into his department, that was strange, if he had been reckoned as one of Kieffer's cases; it could, indeed, be that he had only been 'lodged' there, temporarily, for some reason, and that his interrogation and maltreatment had taken place in an adjacent house. He had been taken in and out of the Avenue Foch so many times, and anyway there had been a communicating corridor. We examined the question closely, going, with care, into the lay-out of the different rooms and corridors, and their relation to staircase, windows, bathroom, etc.

He was pretty sure that the room in which he had been beaten-up was 'one storey down from the top, therefore the fourth' floor of whichever building it was. Now, everything turned on the location of the bathroom in which he had been plunged between beatings, and it was in a different place from that it occupied in 84. He was willing for me to pass the details he had given me to Ernest and discuss them with him in the endeavour to narrow down the site. I realised during this conversation that he was a very honest man; moderate in speech, careful not to state beyond his knowledge of the facts, modest in the best sense, his only concern was that nothing which could be false should go on record.

He had mentioned on the phone that he was in contact with "Archambault's" father, Mr. Maurice Norman, M.B.E. (former President of the British Chamber of Commerce in Paris and member of a distinguished firm of chartered accountants.) Now he told me that although he had known Mr. Norman for years, professionally, and had always known that he had lost a son in these operations, he had only realised just before he came over to England for this surgical operation that that son was "Archambault." Someone had shown him the newspaper which was running *The Starr Affair*, and he had shown it to

Norman as 'another case of smearing,' because Norman had told him his son's name had suffered damage. Norman had exclaimed, 'Why there's something about my son in it,' putting his finger on the name of "Archambault."

Yeo-Thomas had sat next to "Archambault" (Gilbert Norman, as he now knew him to be) in the Black Maria whilst travelling from the Avenue Foch to Fresnes. "Archambault" had told him he had given the first half[11] of his security check only to his interrogator and a reply had come from London: *You forgot your double-security-check. Be more careful.* (I had heard this story for the first time from Starr, later from Ernest, and now I heard it for the third time from Yeo-Thomas. That these three should have given, separately and independently, identical accounts was a tribute to the accuracy of all three.)

Yeo-Thomas thought the father, who had suffered very much, would be grateful if I got in contact with him; for my part also I realised this might be important. "Prosper" and "Archambault" had existed for me as mere codenames, with neither real names nor personal backgrounds attached. To be

---

[11] The security-check was a deliberate spelling mistake which must come up in the clear when the message was deciphered in London. The messages were inscribed on squared paper numbered across and down as in a crossword puzzle and it was the co-ordinates of the square in which the spelling mistake must appear that were individual to each agent. For a fuller exposition of this, see the Epilogue by H. M. G. Lauwers to H. J. Giskes's book *London Calling North Pole*. As "Archambault" had a double security-check he had to make two spelling mistakes in two squares to be indicated by two sets of co-ordinates. If a single one only appeared, therefore, his security-check was incomplete. These individual security-checks, additional to the cipher, were supposed to be the agent's way of showing he was still at liberty. Every radio operator was told before leaving London that if his check failed to appear in any message he would be deemed to be captive, working under German control.

able to write to "Archambault's" father was indeed a step forward.

On the subject of misplaced suspicions, Yeo-Thomas told me a personal story. In March, 1943, he and another officer had been going into Tours, when a man belonging to the "French Section" had come to them to warn them, unofficially, that instructions had been given his group to ambush Yeo-Thomas in Tours and kill him, since he was supposed to be an *agent provocateur* (i.e. German agent).

Yeo-Thomas and his companion took this seriously and went to Nievre instead of Tours.

I was very much astounded by this story, and had to remind myself who it was who was speaking: not some poor bit of riff-raff who could be 'rubbed out' without his loss being missed, but Wing-Commander Yeo-Thomas who wore some of the highest decorations this country can bestow, the George Cross and the Military Cross, and whose reputation stood so high that question of it seemed inconceivable.

Barbara Yeo-Thomas now came in and joined us for a drink; and then they had to move off to somewhere else. They invited me to keep in touch with them, and Yeo-Thomas suggested one or two other people I might contact, including André Simon, the wine merchant, who had been in S.O.E. "French Section" and could tell some interesting stories.

I saw André Simon on September 29th. I still do not know what stories Yeo-Thomas had in mind when he sent me to Simon, but the one that came tumbling out, as my glass was generously filled and refilled with champagne, was not, I think, on the expected list. A woman in the top office of the "French Section" had insisted, in conversation with Simon, so Simon told me, that a certain man was a traitor. 'I have proof!' she had said to Simon.

Had I ever heard of the man in question, Simon asked me?

'No,' I said, unaware that he had named "Gilbert" by his real name.

Simon seemed almost surprised that I had never heard of a personage who had, as he assured me, been the subject of a great deal of discussion. He, Simon, was not convinced of his guilt. The man was certainly not a coward; he had made a number of parachute jumps into France, on one occasion on to a ground that was practically swamp. Coming down by parachute, however gently, one always hit the earth's surface with a certain impetus, and there was the risk that he might strike a boggy patch and be sucked downward. Only a remarkably brave man would, with his eyes open, have agreed to be dropped over a ground which held such a danger. He was a rascal, of course. He had declared quite frankly to Simon that he served with the Section only for the money. 'Your people pay me well; that's the only reason why I work for them.' Those were his own words. He was very candid. There was no hypocrisy about him. But he, Simon, would never believe him a traitor unless he were shown the proof. He did not believe he would send people to their *deaths* for money. He would have a glass of wine with him any day.

Without realising that this appraisal related to "Gilbert", I asked Simon what had happened to the man of whom he was speaking.

Oh, he had had a bit of trouble after the war, but had probably found his feet again by this time.

Yeo-Thomas's former colleagues in R.F. were meanwhile showing me kindness in putting me into contact with further members of that Section, and on October 19th I was driven down to a little gathering at a country house. They had something to tell me concerning Signals. The incoming messages from the field, from France, Holland, Belgium, etc., had all been received by the Royal Corps of Signals, which also did the deciphering. The deciphered messages were brought up to London every day, by special messenger on a motor bicycle, and delivered to the offices of the different national Sections in envelopes marked for the attention of the head of the Section concerned. The words SECURITY CHECK ABSENT were always printed (in capital letters if they remembered rightly) at the bottom of any message not found to bear it, and any mistakes or irregularities in 'sending' noticed by the receiving officer were also noted. A very complete picture was therefore received in London, and in R.F. Section warnings from the Royal Corps of Signals had always been heeded. It seemed unlikely that the Royal Corps of Signals would have been less conscientious in the work it submitted to the British directed "French Section" and "Dutch Section" than in that which it did for R.F. (*Republique Française*).

In view of the disquiet caused by the publication of Colonel Giskes's book, *London Calling North Pole*, and augmented by *The Starr Affair*, concerning the apparent failure in London to note the absence of security checks in messages coming in from the field and now known to have been sent by the Germans over the circuits of the operators they had captured, these members of R.F. Section thought it only fair the public should know that the fault did not lie with the Signals Corps; they thought it desirable that they should say this, since it might be impossible for the men of the Signals Corps to speak up for themselves.

I had by this time entered into correspondence with Mr. Norman, whose address Yeo-Thomas had given me. From his letters I gathered that he was unhappy at the paucity of information concerning his son available from official quarters.[12]

---

[12] Like "Madeleine's" mother, he received the first intimation that his

I wrote to tell him that I was in contact with Ernest who had conducted the interrogation of his son at the Avenue Foch and who would probably be both willing and able to set his mind at rest concerning some of the questions to which, in view of the damaging charges to which his son's name was subject in some quarters, he was seeking an answer.

I told Mr. Norman that if he liked to write a letter to Ernest asking the questions that were on his mind, and send it to me, I would forward it.

He did this. I sent the letter on, and in due course received from Ernest the carbon copy of the reply which he had posted to Mr. Norman direct. It was a nice letter, saying 'I have never considered "Prosper", "Archambault" or any of their colleagues as traitors,' and going on to give some details such as he thought would comfort a father. To me, Ernest wrote that the names of "Gilbert" and of Gilbert Norman, alias "Archambault", had been frequently confused, and that in his opinion the confusion had done the latter no good. He would talk to me further about the case of Mr. Norman's son, together with that of the other "Gilbert", when I came to Germany.

Next, Mr. Norman paid a visit to London and on October 21st brought to my flat a suitcase containing five files concerning his son which he touchingly confided to me. There was a great deal of material on them and they took me some time to go through. I discovered that Gilbert Norman had been born on April 17th, 1915, at St. Cloud, and educated entirely in France; later he had been apprenticed to the London office of the same firm of chartered accountants as his father

---

child might be missing only in May, 1944; both had up to then been receiving periodical messages from the Department in London assuring them that all was well.

belonged to in Paris; when war broke out he had been mobilised in 1940 and later in the year commissioned in the Durham Light Infantry; from January 1941 until April 1942 he was attached as Liaison Officer to the Polish Army Middle East; he was then transferred to S.O.E. "French Section" for training as a wireless operator, and, on November 1st, 1942, parachuted into the Touraine district, with the code-name of "Archambault", to take up duties as wireless operator and second in command to "Prosper"; he had held the rank of Major, been arrested on June 24th, 1943, and been shot at Mauthausen Extermination Camp on September 6th, 1944.

There was also on Mr. Norman's files a number of letters from a Mr. William Suttill, and as I studied them I realised suddenly that he must be "Prosper's" brother. It was, in fact, from these letters that I first learned "Prosper's" real name. Ernest had, in truth, told me that "Prosper" had, when asked, given a name with this sound; but he could not remember the spelling with certainty and, though he could not recollect a 'b' I had privately suspected a pun on the word 'subtle' if, perhaps, "Prosper" had not thought it necessary to tell the Germans his true name. There was, however, no pun; here in the brother's letters was the full name set out, Francis Alfred Suttill.

I now wrote to Mr. William Suttill, to whom Mr. Norman told me he had already posted a copy of *The Starr Affair*, and received an informative reply. Their father was an Englishman, bom in Manchester, who had settled in Lille, married the Frenchwoman who became their mother, built up a flourishing import business and become Chairman of the Chamber of Commerce. Francis had been born at their home in the environs of Lille on March 17th, 1910; he had been sent to England to be educated at Stoneyhurst, returned to France to take a Law degree at the University of Lille, and then gone back to England to continue his Law studies at the University of London. When the war came he was in Chambers at Lincoln's Inn and was believed to have before him a career as an international barrister. He went into the East Surrey Regiment, from which he was afterwards transferred to S.O.E. "French Section" and was, as I knew, in October 1942 parachuted into France to take over the direction of the network destined to bear his name and to become the most important of the "French Section" networks in France. I knew already that he had been arrested on June 24th, 1943, and beyond that practically nothing further was known; the time and manner of his death had not been established with precision but, wrote his brother, according to the War Office statement he had been last seen at Sachsenhausen[13] Concentration Camp on March 18th, 1945, and was officially presumed to have been killed on or shortly after that date.[14]

On Mr. Norman's files were a number of letters which had passed, from 1948 onwards, between himself and Mr. Suttill in discussion of the action to be taken in respect of three books by the priest and historian, the Abbé Paul Guillaume, in which it was alleged that "Prosper" and "Archambault" had collaborated with the enemy. Whilst in French law a libel action in respect of the dead was in some circumstances possible to a member of the family of the deceased, and they might therefore have been able to institute proceedings on behalf of their brother and son respectively, they had been

---

[13] Starr never saw or heard of "Prosper" whilst at Sachsenhausen, but of course Starr was transferred from Sachsenhausen to Mauthausen on February 17th, 1945.

[14] The Supplement to the *London Gazette* dated November 15th, 1945, carries the announcement of the award of the D.S.O. to Major (temporary) Francis Alfred Suttill ["Prosper"]. As the D.S.O. cannot be awarded posthumously, there would appear to be some anomaly.

unable to obtain from the British authorities any information such as would enable them to refute the charges, and, after some correspondence with the Abbé's superiors and others concerned, eventually decided to let the matter drop. They kept their own faith in the son and the brother they had lost.

Side by side in Mr. Norman's files with the issue between himself and the Abbé ran papers relating to a parallel feud between two Frenchmen of the "Prosper" network, the organisers of the sub-sections of North and South Touraine, Maurice Lequeux and Pierre Culioli, who appeared in alignment with Norman and the Abbé respectively. One of Mr. Norman's letters to London implied a regret that his son had not carried out an order given him before he left London to administer a lethal pill to Culioli, who would meet him on the field when he landed by parachute, but who was suspected of treason; "Archambault", it appeared, had felt compunction and, instead of seeking an occasion to administer the pill, had told Culioli about it. I noticed that the reply Mr. Norman received from London to this letter bore no reference to this passage!

After thus being saved by Norman's son, Culioli had been established by "Prosper" as chief of an important section of his network, between Tours and Orleans. In this capacity he had carried on, apparently satisfactorily, until his arrest by the Germans on June 21st, 1943. Whichever way one looked at it, it was perplexing.

There were several aged French newspapers bearing reports of the trials after the war of both Lequeux and Culioli on charges of collaboration with the enemy. Lequeux had been arrested by the Germans on July 1st, 1943, and, after interrogation, had been sent to Auschwitz Extermination Camp. On his return to France in 1945 he found himself charged with having, after capture, given further people belonging to his own group into the hands of the Germans. On October 18th, 1945, he had been judged guilty by the *Cours de Justice* of Orleans, and sentenced to ten years hard labour, with confiscation of goods and national indignity. He had, however, quite soon been released as *gracié* and early in 1947 received official notification of a decree dated July 2nd, 1945, rescinding that of national indignity and confiscation of goods. In his earliest statements he had, feeling himself a victim of the pact, put all the blame on "Archambault"; but now his opinion had changed and it was as the defender of the memory of "Archambault" that he presented himself to Mr. Norman. He now saw Culioli, who had been arrested three days before "Prosper" and "Archambault" as having betrayed them; Culioli, he assured the father was the author of all their troubles.

Culioli was now charged, and one of the newspapers bore a caption in headlines: THE MAN WHO MADE CHURCHILL TREMBLE. Beneath it was a photograph of Culioli looking very small and wistful in large spectacles. The article below averred that Winston Churchill had, in 1943, made a speech in 'secret session of the House of Lords' (sic) to the effect that the invasion had had to be 'put back a year' owing to 'the treason of X.'[15] Culioli, stated the article, was certainly the man to whom Mr. Churchill referred as X.

At the trial of Culioli, Lequeux had been an important witness for the prosecution. The verdict had been expressed in somewhat equivocal terms; Culioli had applied for retrial, and the higher court at which this was heard had found him 'Not Guilty.'

---

[15] Not to be confused with the character whom I referred to as X in my first two books.

If Ernest was right, and the whole "Prosper" network had in fact been betrayed by "Gilbert", this ado might, I felt, have been unnecessary. I told Mr. Norman my premonition about this for, whilst he still believed, following Lequeux, that Culioli had betrayed his son, I suspected that the acquittal might have been just.

By November 11th, 1954, I was at last free to travel to Germany and see Ernest again after an interval of over four years.

CHAPTER THREE: ERNEST'S STATEMENT

After a journey lasting over twenty-four hours, I was met on the platform, on the evening of Friday, November 12th, by Ernest and his wife, a Frenchwoman who had, at the time of my first visit to Germany, not yet been released by the authorities. One each side of me and talking eagerly, they led me, on foot for I was stiff with travelling, through the streets of the old-world town to the hotel where they had booked me a room, and as soon as I had dumped my case, across the road to their place. I had eaten on the train, but they had a bottle of wine waiting for me and — in my honour, a beverage for which they had little taste themselves — tea.

I had not really thought that Ernest would want to talk about "Gilbert" this evening. I knew it was a subject that would be distasteful to him. However, he opened it himself, but with some cautionary remarks. It was a very difficult, indeed an impossible, matter on which to speak except in private, since "Gilbert" had been acquitted. He also wished to make clear, right at the beginning, that even in the event of the charge being re-opened, as was in some circumstances possible under French law, he would not go to Paris to give evidence against him. They would have to make do with his old statement, which was still on their files. He had not departed from his principle, which he had expressed at our very first meeting, that it was unfitting for a German to give evidence against an Allied national who had worked for Germany, for the purpose of enabling the Allied authorities to obtain a prosecution; unless it was the case, that suspicion must otherwise fall on an innocent person. That was the only reason why he had gone into the box to give evidence in a certain case of which I knew. It was likewise the only reason why he had, in 1949, at the request of the French authorities, made a statement concerning "Gilbert"; he had been given to understand that a number of other persons, both living and dead, lay under suspicion, a suspicion which could not be dissipated unless he disclosed the facts within his knowledge. It was solely because he understood from me that a cloud did still hang over French and British persons, both living and dead, whom he knew to be innocent, that he was prepared to make a statement to me now.

He told me the real name of "Gilbert." I realised now for the first time that this was the man of whom André Simon had talked to me, the man who had been suspected by some but who had shown bravery in making a parachute jump on to swampy ground. Ernest had not known "Gilbert's" real name until after the war, when the French authorities in Paris told him in 1949. Previously he had thought that "Gilbert" was an Englishman, although they spoke with him in French. He could not recollect how he had got this idea, and the French authorities had satisfied him it was not correct, and that "Gilbert" was in fact French. There was, Ernest thought, not the smallest doubt about the identification established by the authorities in Paris, but he would call the agent of whom he knew "Gilbert", because it came more natural.

He had first heard of him as BOE 48; this was the reference which always appeared, added in pencil or pen on the corner of the photostatted copies of the mail, sent by "Prosper" and "Archambault" from the field to London. BOE stood for Boemelburg, S.S. Sturmbannführer Karl Boemelburg, chief of the Gestapo in Paris, who had his H.Q. next door to them at

82 Avenue Foch. The reference mark meant that he was the 48th agent on Boemelburg's register. It was Kieffer who always gave the photostatted reports to Ernest, and who told him that they had been sent over from Boemelburg's office because they concerned the "French Section"; all "French Section" matters were handled by Kieffer. It was likewise Kieffer who told him that BOE 48 was the Air Movements Officer for the "French Section" for the whole of occupied France, responsible for finding and preparing fields suitable for parachute drops and for landing of aircraft and for meeting and seeing off agents and aircraft; that amongst his other duties was that of receiving mail from those who wished to send it to London by departing aircraft and putting it aboard the same; that before putting it aboard he submitted it to Boemelburg's office where the photostats were made, after which the mail was given back to him to put on the aircraft bound for London; and that the code-name of BOE 48 with his chiefs in London was "Gilbert."

Later, when Boemelburg was transferred to Vichy, "Gilbert" had been attached to Kieffer's department direct, and Dr. Goetz had been deputed to be his contact. Now, through Goetz, they heard more of him, in a personal way, since Goetz would sometimes describe the interviews he had had with him; so far Ernest knew, they always met outside.

He himself had only met "Gilbert" once, right at the end, when he was due to go back to London. Kieffer had never really trusted "Gilbert." He was accustomed to say, 'He betrays the English and his own compatriots to us; he would betray us to them the day it suited him better.' The fact that "Gilbert" had been recalled to London suggested that London had become suspicious of his activities; and now that he was really going, Kieffer suspected that he might attempt some mischief, such as the kidnapping of Goetz, if he perhaps brought a 'friend' to help him, in order to take Goetz with him to London as a hostage against Kieffer's silence concerning his own activities. To safeguard Goetz, Kieffer had therefore sent Ernest with him to the last interview with "Gilbert." This had lasted for only a few minutes; "Gilbert" had given them the B.B.C. message which would be broadcast from London to announce his safe arrival. A few days later they heard it.

That was all Ernest told me the first night. But, concisely and without frills, it was the whole story in a nutshell. The events he had disclosed were so momentous that it scarcely seemed credible they had taken so few minutes to relate. I think for a moment he saw the humour of it, for he said, 'So little — and so much.'

With that to think about, I regained my hotel and went to bed. In the morning I wrote it out. In the afternoon (being Saturday he was free in the afternoon) I took it over to their flat and showed him what I had written down and asked him to go over it. He began doing so; then suddenly he said he would write it out himself. Then he would know that it was correct and that any nuances it might contain were those for which he himself was responsible.

When I had first written to him about "Gilbert" he had replied that he could not put anything about this on paper; that he should now offer to do so was an enormous step forward. I waited whilst he went over to his desk and wrote for some time, in pencil, on thin sheets of foolscap paper. Then he gave them to me. He had written (I translate from his French):

It was not until after the arrest of "Prosper", "Archambault" and their collaborators (on June 24th, 1943) that Kieffer gave me for the first time photostats of documents bearing the reference "BOE 48" and it was not until some time after that I learnt from him that "BOE 48" (Agent 48 of Boemelburg), was one "Gilbert" responsible for the landings of British aircraft in the occupied zone of France. "Gilbert" was charged by the French Section with the duty of selecting landing-grounds, organising the landing of aircraft, receiving the agents who landed by these aircraft, putting those due to return to London on board homeward-bound aircraft and forwarding by the same aircraft the mail of the agents of the French Section.

Up to the end of 1943, "Gilbert" was the agent of Boemelburg, Chief of the Gestapo in France, and came directly under him. At the time of the departure of Boemelburg for Vichy, towards the end of 1943 or early in 1944, he became the agent of Kieffer and worked immediately under him. However, I never saw "Gilbert" in our office in the Avenue Foch. It was Goetz who made the liaison between Kieffer and "Gilbert" and their meetings took place outside our own office.

In fact I only saw him once, shortly before his return to London in February, 1944. Kieffer had never entirely trusted him and told me to accompany Goetz to a meeting with him as a precaution, since he was afraid that "Gilbert" might have Goetz kidnapped and carry him off to London. The meeting took place in an empty apartment not far from the Arc de Triomphe. Goetz had a key to it. "Gilbert" came alone and confirmed that he was going to London. He said he thought he was under suspicion. He gave Goetz the B.B.C. code message which would announce his arrival there. A few days afterwards we heard this message broadcast by the B.B.C.

Later we arrested Robert Bennoist,[16] alias "Lionel," a French officer of the French Section, who told me that he had travelled back to London in the same aircraft as "Gilbert" and that in London he had been questioned about him by the British Security Service, which suspected "Gilbert" of being a traitor. Robert Bennoist told me that he had testified in favour of "Gilbert" as he had no reason to suppose that he was a traitor. He asked me if "Gilbert" was really in relation with us. I did not answer him. "Gilbert" had a "letter-box" in Paris where he or his courier, "Claire" received agents and the mail for the agents of the French Section for the whole of the occupied zone of France. The "letterbox" and the meetings in a café in Paris became known to Kieffer, though I presume that meetings must also have been held in places that we did not know about.

We came to know of "Gilbert's" landing-ground near Angers and Kieffer was from time to time aware of B.B.C. messages which gave warning of forthcoming landings. "Gilbert" passed on to Kieffer some of the mail and information about the arrival of aircraft. In return, he obtained a promise that the Germans would never shoot down or capture any of the aircraft landing on his landing-grounds. Thus he could receive and despatch aircraft with a perfectly easy mind (*en toute tranquillité*). The British agents' mail for London, which "Gilbert" passed on to Kieffer, was photographed by our service and then returned to "Gilbert," who sent it on to London. I do not suppose that he passed over the entire mail to Kieffer.

---

[16] Hanged at Buchenwald, September 10th, 1944.

"Prosper," "Archambault" and their collaborators were arrested as the result of reports, intended for London, which "Gilbert" had passed over to Boemelburg. After their arrest, Kieffer handed to me photographic copies of the reports that "Prosper" and "Archambault" had sent to London. They contained almost complete information about their activities, together with addresses and names. It was these reports which enabled us to bring off our great round-up (*coup de filet*) of the "Prosper" organisation.

As I read this over with him, I asked him some questions and he gave me some supplementary information.

Had he ever heard if "Gilbert" was paid by the Germans, I asked him?

No, he had, as a matter of fact, never heard money mentioned in connection with "Gilbert." He thought it would be improper to speculate on the motive which had inspired him to render these services to the Germans. Nevertheless, he thought it was probably one of self-interest. He had never heard it suggested that it was genuine love of Germany or in any sense ideological. Kieffer had regarded "Gilbert" purely as a rascal, a man with no genuine loyalty anywhere.

I asked him why Kieffer had allowed "Gilbert" to return to England.

He could not remember Kieffer making any specific pronouncement of his reasons. His own interpretation of Kieffer's decision, which he thought represented the general 'climate' of thought at the Avenue Foch, was that if they prevented "Gilbert" from going back, London would *know* that he had gone over to the Germans; unless they thought he had been arrested. In either case, they would know that he was no longer functioning as their Air Movements Officer and would appoint a new one, whose identity would be unknown to Kieffer's service and whose operations would escape their supervision. "Gilbert" had hopes that if he went back to brazen it out he would be able to think of some story to tell his chiefs in London to convince them that their suspicions were unfounded. If he succeeded, he might be allowed to return. Even if he did not return and a new man was appointed in his stead, the new man might be permitted to use the same landing-fields and letterboxes, if "Gilbert" had been able to satisfy London that there had not been a leak, and thus they would be able to keep tabs on him. If they detained "Gilbert" they lost *everything*; if they let him go, they lost, indeed, those services which he had been accustomed to render to their department, but they retained the hope of being able to 'supervise' (unseen) the activities of his successor.

In fact, this hope was realised. "Gilbert" told them at the last interview (the one at which Ernest had been present) that a man already in the field, whose code-name was "Marc," had been appointed to take over from him and would use the same facilities. To the best of his knowledge, "Marc" had never been instructed to find any airfields other than those he had 'inherited' from "Gilbert" and thus, though "Marc" never entered into relations with their department, they were able, from the shadows as it were, to keep to some extent abreast of his operations.

He should have said — though he had not the heart to re-write his statement to include this — that a few days prior to this last interview, when he already knew that he was going, "Gilbert" had given them the expected time of arrival of three agents from London on his field at Angers. Contrary to usual practice, Kieffer had insisted, since it was so near to the end, on having two of his own men on the field as part of the reception committee. (Normally, he believed, they were trailed only from the railway station nearest the field or some other convenient point). In the train Kieffer's two men had a bit of worry. The three men from London insisted (pathetically in the circumstances) on splitting up and sitting in separate compartments at some distance from each other 'for security'. This gave Kieffer's two some anxiety in that they had to walk up and down the corridor continually to make sure that they were all still there and that no one of them had got off at an intermediate station. When they got out at Paris, however, the three had joined up again on the platform and had been arrested by a team taking-over from the two who had followed them up.

He, himself, had once visited the field at Angers, but not in company with "Gilbert."

When he said that he and Goetz had met "Gilbert" in an 'empty' apartment, did he mean literally empty, I asked?

Yes, literally. No covering on the floor-boards and not a single item of furniture. Not even a chair to sit down on. It was between the Arc de Triomphe and the Bois de Boulogne; not far from the Avenue Foch, in fact, and in a street somewhere behind 'their' side of it. He could not remember the name of the street; as Goetz had led him there, he had not noticed in particular. He had the impression that "Gilbert" was slightly disconcerted that Goetz should come accompanied by a second man, probably because the unexplained additional presence implied distrust.

'What was Gilbert *like*?' I asked. 'What impression did he make on you as a person when you met him?'

He smiled with a slight irony. He made what, in any other circumstances, would have been a good impression. His clothes were good. Cloth of a good quality. Well cut. Not loud.

He had 'a good presence'; his manner was that of a man accustomed to being well received. Body well-built, though slender; even the face 'quite agreeable.' Quite tall, that is, nearly as tall as Ernest himself. His bearing, as he stood talking with them, showed no consciousness of the shame of what he was doing. 'It was hard to realise that he was what he was. One would have said, a gentleman.'

How had "Gilbert" come to be acquitted, I asked?

He did not know the precise circumstances. He had only gathered in Paris — after he made his deposition soon after his arrival in 1949 — that it must have been some time previously. He had been asked to make depositions concerning a number of persons of Allied nationality. In due course, he had been asked to make one concerning "Gilbert." The *Juge d'Instruction* before whom he made it had received it in silence. It was only a day or two later that one of the other *Juges* had said to him 'It's a pity we did not have your testimony earlier. He was tried and acquitted some time ago. If we had had your evidence then, the verdict might have been different.'

He had gathered from odd remarks made by various of the *Juges* that the acquittal had been due to a British intervention on the behalf of "Gilbert." But he did not know what form it had taken. He was certain only that the French felt exceedingly bitter about it and suspected "London" or the "Intelligence Service" of having arranged the whole thing in an interest not disclosed to their French allies.

That there was not a perfect 'alignment' between London and Paris, he had realised from an earlier episode. He had been captured, in the first place, by the Americans, in Bavaria and held at Dachau; on April 1st, 1947, he had been collected from there by the British and taken to the British internment camp at Staumühle, near Paderborn in Westphalia. Since they knew his identity and that he had been Kieffer's interpreter, he had expected now to be subjected to a rigorous questioning about the Avenue Foch. Nothing of the sort, however, materialised. They asked him questions about his birth, home background and upbringing and why he had left Germany as a young man to settle in France. Apart from that they only asked him broad questions of an administrative nature: what was the difference between *Sicherheitsdienst* and *Sicherheitspolizei*, and did they, like the *Geheimstaatspolizei* come under the *Reichssicherheitshauptamt?* And, if so, how were these services related? These were questions to which he scarcely knew the answer himself, and they could surely have found a better informant. To this day, he would hesitate to draw up a 'family-tree' setting out the relations of all these services, which were very complicated.

Concerning his experiences at the Avenue Foch, on the other hand, they showed no desire to know anything at all. They had never enquired the extent of his knowledge of Kieffer's service. They had asked no questions relative to operations. They had asked nothing about any of the prisoners who had been brought in — with the solitary exception of Starr, against whom they had sought an adverse deposition. The name of no other prisoner had been so much as spoken. In due course he was told that his examination had been completed and that he would be released about the middle of the month (July, 1947).

About the 17th or 18th July, he was, instead of being released, sent back to the Americans. The Americans, who had evidently not been warned, and did not want a man they had already cleared, asked him if he knew for what purpose he had been returned to them. He did not. As the British, apparently, would not have him back and the Americans did not want to keep him, they sent him again to Dachau, which had now reverted to German hands, for examination by the German "De-Nazification" authorities. These at last informed him, in April 1948, that they had finished with him and he was free to go. It was unfortunate that he was, at the time when this communication was brought to him, ill in bed in the camp infirmary. A fortnight later when he was able to get up and was gathering his things together to go, he was told that his release had been cancelled. No reason was given. At the beginning of May he was taken back to the British camp at Staumühle and told he must remain there to be at the disposal of a German tribunal to which the British authorities had handed his file; and on June 30th he was discharged from the camp on condition that he did not leave the British zone. On September 13th, he was at last given a complete clearance and freed to go where he liked. (The British had still not asked him any questions about the Avenue Foch.)

On December 20th he was at last able to go to his home, or rather his family's home, which was in the French zone, and of course reported his arrival to the German authorities, who, in their turn informed the French. The French authorities showed considerably more interest in him; and in January, 1949, a French officer arrived from Baden-Baden to see him, and he was thoroughly questioned. All this time his wife being a Frenchwoman was still in Rennes prison; convinced of her innocence of collaboration with his department, and hoping to be able to help her if he could get to Paris, he offered to place himself at the disposal of the French authorities in Paris. He then received instructions to present himself at the frontier, which he did at the end of April, 1949; there he was taken over by a French military escort which conducted him to Paris and to the prison in the *rue de Cherche Midi*, where he was kept except when required for questioning.

When brought up to the *Tribunal Militaire*, practically the first
words with which his *Juge d'Instruction*, Captain Desquivres,
greeted him were, 'So, you are a British agent.'

Quite astonished by this charge, he denied it with indignation
and asked Captain Desquivres whatever had given him such an
idea.

'We have no proof,' replied Desquivres, and passed him a file
on which was the carbon of a letter written by the French
authorities to the British in the first fortnight of July 1947,
saying they understood the British were now finishing with
him (Ernest) and would be glad if, when they had done so,
they would hand him over to them (the French.) Then
Desquivres had flipped over the page and shown him the reply
which had been received from the British authorities; it stated
that he was not in British hands and that they had no
knowledge of his whereabouts. It was dated just a day or so
after his mysterious transfer to the Americans, who having
discharged him once already, did *not* want him back. The
French letter must have been received whilst he was still in
British hands, and he must have been sent to the Americans
between its receipt and the dating of the reply. 'If you are not a
British agent, why did they want to keep you from us?' asked
Desquivres.

He spoke the truth when he said he did not know. But it
became quite obvious that the French believed that he had
been deliberately withheld from them in order that they should
not be able to examine him and ask his testimony on various
matters. In March 1950 he got his *Non Lieu.*

Remembering some words of two D.S.T.[17] men to whom I
had been introduced by Starr, I recognised this portrait of
French feelings.

---

[17] D.S.T. *Department de la Surveillance du Territoire*, the French security

We talked all through the afternoon, evening, night and into the early hours of the morning; indeed, we must have talked about twelve hours at a stretch broken only for a short spell for eating.

We came to "Prosper" and "Archambault" and the pact. He had told me about the pact a long time ago, but only in so far as concerned "Prosper" and without full relation to its background.

The mail had given Kieffer's department pretty complete information concerning the overall lay-out and organisation of the giant "Prosper" network. They knew the identities of its principle members, the chiefs of its main sub-sectors and the "letter-boxes" they used. When "Prosper" and "Archambault" were confronted with the photostats of the long and detailed reports they had sent to London and realised the extent of Kieffer's knowledge, they were aghast. They knew that they had been betrayed. They could see quite clearly that the arrests would not stop with their own persons as Kieffer's department was in a position to extend them over a wide area in only a little time. Now Kieffer proposed the pact to "Prosper." If "Prosper" would save his department trouble by disclosing the addresses at which the arms were stored, Kieffer would in return guarantee that neither he nor any of his colleagues, already captured or later to be captured, would — despite the fact that they were enemy agents working in plain clothes — be killed or ill-treated.

"Prosper", deeply troubled, asked what authority Kieffer had to offer such a guarantee. Ernest translated his question. No one else was present; only "Prosper", Kieffer and himself as intermediary. What assurance, "Prosper" asked, could Kieffer

---

office combining functions equivalent to those in this country divided between M.I.5 and Scotland Yard Special Branch.

give him that if he accepted the terms of this pact, they would be maintained on the German side?

Kieffer replied that he would apply to Berlin for the authority; and he did so. The authority was sent; a paper setting out the terms of the pact as proposed by Kieffer and bearing the stamp of the *Reichssicherheitshauptamt*. It was as official as anything could be. "Prosper" read it very carefully, and decided to accept it. He was a loyal English gentleman, and he did it, Ernest felt sure, only for the lives of the men and women under his command. Of the three who had been present at that solemn moment, only he was alive to testify to the spirit in which the pact was concluded. He had no doubt that "Prosper" was deeply aware of its gravity and that his motive was pure. He was not a man who would have been afraid to die. He had no doubt, equally, that Kieffer had been as sure as he had been himself that the pact would be upheld loyally upon the German side. It was perhaps his faith and Kieffer's which had communicated itself to "Prosper."

When the pact had been signed, "Archambault" was brought in and "Prosper" told him what he had done. As his commanding officer, until their capture, he advised him to stand by the terms of it and to give what co-operation was necessary in their carrying out.

After that, "Prosper" was taken away from the Avenue Foch (he heard he was sent to Berlin) and "Archambault" alone was retained. Upon him devolved the painful duty of carrying through the measures "Prosper" had authorised and explaining what had taken place to other prisoners as they were brought in. It was an unenviable position. Some of those to whom he had to explain it took it amiss. Ignorant of what had taken place, and confronted with "Archambault" in his ungrateful role, some thought that it was "Archambault" who had betrayed them. "Archambault" for his part, dared not give the Germans the pretext to say that the terms had not been carried out from the British side; nobody could have been put into a more thankless position.

There was another thing, more grave. Both "Prosper" and "Archambault" were convinced that the betrayal came from London.[18] They had already suspected the treason of "Gilbert", but believed there was also treason from the top office. He (Ernest) could not know whether they were right, but in any case it was not his part, as Kieffer's interpreter, to question a conviction which tended to play them into German hands; it was their own conviction; neither he nor Kieffer suggested it to them. And it was this conviction on the part of "Prosper" and "Archambault" that they had been betrayed from London, which constituted the real nightmare of their position. Whereas betrayal from below might generate only anger at having been deceived by a subordinate, the suspicion of betrayal from above undermined the basis of confidence. It was worse because they did not seem to know, themselves, exactly whom they suspected, and were groping in their attempt to understand things. Bewildered, betrayed and cut off from the possibility of enlightenment, "Prosper" and "Archambault" were in a desolate position.

It was not in the very least that they wished to play the German game, but in the appalling isolation in which they found themselves they had felt the need of placing confidence in *someone* even if it was the enemy. Kieffer and he had treated them with consideration and, even if "Prosper" and "Archambault" loathed them as "Gestapo", Ernest thought he

---

[18] This, for me, was confirmation of what Madame Balachowsky, of the "Prosper" network, had told me of her conversations with "Prosper" just before he was arrested. See *The Starr Affair*.

was not wrong in feeling that, as Germans serving their own country, they were less repugnant to "Prosper" and "Archambault" than those by whom they believed they had been betrayed. As they were completely in Kieffer's hands, they had come to feel that the best thing they could do was to trust him. Apart from anything else, they wanted to remain alive in order to return to England after the war (which they were still convinced England would win) to lay the position before their own authorities and demand an enquiry. They said that. There was no doubt in his own mind that had "Prosper" and "Archambault" lived to return to England after the war, they would, in fact, have told all that they knew. As it was, their knowledge had died with them: for they had never told the Germans exactly what it was.

The guarantee had been broken in Germany. He recapitulated what I already knew. It was kept so long as they were in Kieffer's hands. Shortly before the German retreat from France in the summer of 1944 all prisoners had been evacuated to Germany. (They could not be allowed to fall into Allied hands or they would give away what they knew of the radio game.) They passed, then, into other hands; perhaps into the hands of those who did not know even of the existence of the pact. It was not to the honour of Germany. It was the betrayal of the pact which affected Ernest more than anything he had experienced in the war. Deeply loyal to Kieffer, he would not have disclosed the existence of the pact to the French authorities for fear of exposing Kieffer to the suspicion of having acted in bad faith, had he not realised that unless it were known, "Prosper" and "Archambault" must, themselves, appear as mere "*collaborateurs.*" He had felt he owed it to their memories, to the honour of the dead, to explain what had happened. Though as a matter of fact, the French authorities had seemed to know about the pact already, having heard about it from some of those to whom "Archambault" had explained the position and who had survived to tell the tale.

I asked him whether he, himself, believed that they had an agent in London.

He knew no more than he had known in 1943. To prisoners, when they asked, he used to reply, "Perhaps," but he knew no more than they did. It was a very teasing question. He did not know why "Prosper" and "Archambault" had been so set on this idea. On the face of it, there seemed to be no reason to look beyond "Gilbert." He alone sufficed to account for most things. There was only one thing he did not know whether it would be correct to attribute to "Gilbert", though not in itself a very important thing.

They had aerial photographs of some of the training-schools in England. Not of all of them. There were written tabulations of the personnel, etc., of a large number. But there were these photographs of perhaps five or six. There was nothing written on the back except the name of the place. No reference number or other marking to suggest where they came from. They were nothing to look at; just photographs of country houses which might have been anywhere. Kieffer and he had no way of knowing whether they represented the places they were supposed to. But the prisoners, when confronted with them, seemed to recognise them, and so he and Kieffer supposed they must be the genuine article. "Gilbert", in the field, could not have materialised these things out of his hat. He had come from London at the beginning of the year. Nobody knew at what date or how he had been recruited as a German agent. The photographs were of no use. Excepting that, on top of everything else, they added to the dismay of prisoners. They could not have been worth while taking on purpose by a German agent. If they had been brought or sent by a German agent, it could only have been 'for good measure' or to show 'good will', along with matters more important, or indeed instead of matters more important if he had nothing more useful to send or bring. Ernest did not know from what quarter they reached Kieffer.

We had talked until after two in the morning, and with these heavy things to think about I bade them, Ernest and his wife, goodnight and went back to my hotel and bed.

The next day, Sunday, Ernest had the whole day free. In the morning he and his wife took me to an exhibition of flowers being given (in November!) under glass in the park. We had lunch out, then a long walk over the hill at the back of the town; for some time we stood and watched a wild squirrel leaping from branch to branch. During the whole time that we were out, I don't think we mentioned the Avenue Foch. We needed the respite. But once we were back in their flat, the conversation 'settled in' again for the evening.

I mentioned Yeo-Thomas. Ernest said he knew that the *Resistants* and de Gaulle agents were worse treated than the "French Section he had not realised that it was to that point at 86. For he was sure it was 86 that was in question. The name of Yeo-Thomas had been unknown to him until he read *The White Rabbit*, but he knew about Brossolette, whose name he had discovered in the text, having been virtually eye-witness to the accident in which he met his death whilst trying to escape from a window on the top floor. (I asked him to enlarge on this because it had been assumed in a number of books that Brossolette committed suicide.) He had heard a strange scraping noise against the outside of the building, then, after an interval of a moment or so, the same thing at a lower level, and then again lower. Going to the window to see what was happening, he was just in time to see a man fall to the ground. He ran downstairs and out to him and found him, although obviously heavily injured, endeavouring to get to his feet, and said '*Ne bougez pas*!' ('Don't move.') An ambulance was very quickly on the scene, and he went up to find the guard. This guard already had a history; he had been caught more than once asleep on duty; perhaps there was something the matter with him. He taxed him with the words, I suppose you were asleep when this happened! The guard, terrified of being punished, denied it and declared that the prisoner had rushed to the window and hurled himself out with such speed and violence that he had been unable to stop him despite his vigilance. Ernest had not challenged this excuse since he did not want to make trouble for the guard; it might have been severe. He had not, however, a doubt in the world that the guard was lying. Brossolette had neither leaped nor fallen from the fifth floor. He must have climbed out and lowered himself from floor to floor by way of the balconies, which would have made such a descent quite possible to an athletic man, and must have missed his footing on perhaps the second floor and fallen backwards, injuring his spine. He died some time afterwards in the Hôpital de la Pitié. I asked and obtained his permission to make his witness known, since it had been given out that Major Brossolette committed suicide, and suicide is considered by the Church a sin.[19]

Brossolette was one of Schmidt's cases. That he knew for certain. And Dr. Schmidt was in charge of the department at 86, next door. If Yeo-Thomas, as appeared from the text, of

---

[19] 'I wrote to General de Gaulle about this, and received a very nice letter back from the General himself, saying he was much interested by the information I sent him and that he would pass it on to Major Brossolette's widow 'for her comfort.'

The White Rabbit had worked with Brossolette, then Ernest was sure he must have been handled in the same department, since their files would have been considered together. 'Will you ask Mr. Yeo-Thomas for me if the name, Schmidt, means nothing to him?'

This rang a bell for me. I remembered a book *Air Commando*[20] by Serge Vaculik in which the author alleged that in a house on the Avenue Foch (number not given) one fingernail had been extracted from him by a Dr. Schmidt.

We talked again until late into the night. Whilst Ernest would maintain a distinction between the action of a man at liberty, such as "Gilbert", who would seem to be under no compulsion, and the shifts, slips and occasional weaknesses of prisoners, I must, he said, realise that a good deal of information had been drawn from the latter.

We spoke of one or two cases. He had said nothing that was untrue, in any of the depositions he had made to the Allied authorities, but it was not incumbent upon him to volunteer information which could reflect adversely on any of the prisoners who had passed through his hands; sometimes it was possible, without lying, just in the way one worded a paragraph, to give them a little cover. Between the Scylla and Charybdis of false testimony and denunciation, it seemed to him the better part. Appeals to testify concerning the conduct of Allied nationals placed a German in something of a dilemma; it was not so easy to pick one's way with honour. Curiously enough, one of the few who stood in need of no such cover was Starr; nothing had 'slipped' through Starr; he was one of the rare agents of the "French Section" whose arrest had had no distressing consequences for his colleagues.

---

[20] Jarrolds,

In his case, he could, in all sincerity, give an unqualified clearance.

On the semi-eternal question of the radio-game, he told me that even when they retreated from Paris to Nancy in August 1944 they had 'taken back' with them at least two radio 'lines' which they had continued to play-back to London 'fruitfully' (he had mentioned this by letter as a matter of fact); even from Germany, first from Offenburg, then from Freiburg, and finally from near Lake Constance, they had kept it up until April, 1945, that is almost to the end of the war, though by this time it was no longer the "French Section" to which they were working, but an American or Anglo-American service based on London. The last Allied agents to be dropped into Kieffer's hands, as the result of the radio-game, near the shores of Lake Constance, in January 1945, were two Americans, able to speak German, and one apparently real German who had taken service against his own country. They had papers making them out to hold S.S. ranks equivalent to Kieffer's! 'But why are they made out to be valid for only three months ahead?' Kieffer asked one of the false Sturmbannführers; 'Ours are made out for six months ahead.'

'Then they are out of order!' retorted the false Sturmbannführer blandly. 'They have now to be renewed every three months for security!'

Kieffer was sufficiently concerned about this to send Ernest up to Berlin to find out the truth of it, and for the first and only time he met a very high official of their service, to tell this ridiculous story. The prisoners' intelligence was incorrect, this person told him, only to the extent of being a little previous. It was intended to make them renewable every three months but the instructions and the papers made out in the new way had not been issued yet.

So it was not only from London that leaks occurred. This episode introduced a lighter note.

'And do you really intend to publish all that I have told you about "Gilbert"?' Ernest asked me. He was afraid that "Gilbert" would sue me for defamation, since he had been acquitted.

I said I would think about the legal position when the time came, if indeed I found the material to write another book.

CHAPTER FOUR: OLD NEWSPAPER FILES

I travelled back through Paris where I met Starr and also, unexpectedly, his brother, Lt-Col. George Starr, D.S.O., M.C., Légion d'Honneur, etc., who had been one of the successes of the "French Section." He had borne the code-name "Hilaire" and he had been the Organiser of a large network in Gascony (where Marie-Anne Walters, author of *Moondrop in Gascony*, had been his courier), which had been one of the few to survive until the eventual day of the invasion, and to rise according to plan and engage the Germans in fighting. He said he was glad I had written the book about his brother, whom he felt had been treated shabbily.

On the subject of radio sets, he told me that he had had a message sent through his operator warning London that two radio posts of which he knew had become German controlled. The reply he had received was: 'Mind your own business. We know what we are doing.' He supposed they did, though he was at a loss to know what this signified; having transmitted the information, it was not his business to interfere further.

As I could get no further for the moment I returned to England and then on January 6th, 1955, went back to Paris. My first call, the next day, Friday the 7th, was on Yeo-Thomas, now back in his office. I told him about my trip to Germany: in reply to Ernest's question whether the name Schmidt conveyed anything, he replied promptly in the affirmative. A Dr. Schmidt came several times into the room whilst he was being interrogated and spoke with the interrogators, and also put some questions himself. He had not known that he was, in fact, the officer in charge of the department, but then he had never known who was the officer in charge; certainly Schmidt took a prominent part in the proceedings; and he would have no difficulty in believing that it was he. He accepted that he had, in fact, been 'handled' in Schmidt's department. Schmidt, he added, spoke English without a trace of accent and had, before the war, been employed in the Imperial Tobacco Company! He was glad, though not in the least surprised, to hear Ernest's testimony as to the manner of Brossolette's death; he had never believed in the suicide story anyway. The story of "Gilbert" interested him greatly.

During the next few days he went to considerable pains in the endeavour to obtain for me some information concerning the trial of "Gilbert" or at least the date of it. I also tried through my own contacts but equally in vain. There was nothing for it but to read through at least three years of the back numbers of some French newspaper, page by page and column by column, and hope to come upon a report of it.

Tuesday, I took myself to the offices of *France-Soir* in the rue Réaumur, and found their 'ancient numbers' department, and began a search through several years of issues, paragraph by paragraph, column by column, page by page and day by day; this work continued for the rest of the week.

On Saturday Yeo-Thomas put me in contact with Lieut. Gaston Cohen, M.C., alias "Justin" who had worked in the "Prosper" network.

Cohen spoke of Boddington and Agazarian. Major Agazarian, who came of a Mauritian family, was the radio operator Boddington brought out with him when he visited the field in July 1943.[21] Boddington had been supposed to meet

---

[21] This was not the first mission of Major Agazarian. He had been working as radio operator in Paris, Sologne and Vai de Loire for

"Archambault" (who had, of course, been for three weeks in German hands), but had sent Agazarian in his stead to the house in the rue de Rome where the meeting was to take place. There Agazarian was arrested, since it was, of course, the Germans who were waiting.

Cohen had transmitted intelligence of "Archambault's" arrest to London almost as soon as it happened. He had been parachuted in June 1943, as a radio operator to supplement the "Prosper" network, just a few days before the great round-up. On the morning of the 24th, "Archambault" had been supposed to meet him in order to give him, as a newcomer, some instructions. He had waited in the flat where he was supposed to wait; but "Archambault" had not come. It was, in fact, in the early hours of the 24th that "Archambault" had been arrested.[22] He had therefore had it in his power to betray the place of his rendezvous with Cohen; had he turned traitor he could have brought the Germans with him to the rendezvous.

That Cohen had not, in these circumstances, been arrested was, in fact, powerful evidence for "Archambault."

---

some time and was now returning from a brief visit he had made to London. Major Boddington had also visited the South of France in August, 1942.

[22] Between midnight and 00.15 a.m., June 24th, 1943, a party of about fifteen Germans arrived in two cars at the home on the Boulevard Henri-Martin of Monsieur Laurent with whom "Archambault" was staying. According to M. Laurent only one or two came inside at first and asked him to tell his guest they came *'de la part d'"Archambault",'* on the part of "Archambault." M. Laurent, ignorant that this was in fact the code-name of his guest, went upstairs and repeated his message to him literally. "Archambault" got out of bed and came downstairs and was immediately seized. The Germans then went upstairs themselves and found "Denise" in bed. Actually, she was domiciled in the rue des Petites Ecuries but staying here for the night.

Cohen had told his immediate chief, a Swiss, that "Archambault" had not arrived. The Swiss then made cautious investigations to see whether "Archambault" were still at liberty; as he found no sign of life either from him or from "Prosper", he instructed Cohen to transmit a message to London saying, as from himself, that "Prosper" and "Archambault" must be presumed to have been arrested.

I told Cohen that "Madeleine" (who must have been landed about the same time as he was parachuted, but with whom he had had no contact) had also transmitted to London immediate intelligence of the arrest of "Prosper" and "Archambault."[23]

Cohen said the reply which came from London to him, for the Swiss, was: 'You must be mistaken. Archambault is still transmitting to us.' The Swiss had then instructed Cohen to send a message saying that if "Archambault" was still transmitting it could only be for the Germans, since he was certainly in German hands.

I had heard this story before. Ernest had told me that a Swiss Organiser of the "French Section" whom they had captured had asked his permission to speak with "Archambault." "Archambault" was, at that time, in the Hôpital de la Pitié, having been, at some time during the winter 1943-44, shot down whilst attempting to escape; it was when he was taken down the stairs to the prison van which should have transported him to Fresnes that he made a spurt down the pavement and somebody shot him in the leg. Ernest took the Swiss into the ward where "Archambault" lay in bed and told him he might speak with him subject to the condition that he,

---

[23] According to the *Official Citation* for the posthumous award of the George Cross to Noor Inayat Khan ("Madeleine"), she was left after these arrests 'the last remaining link with London.' That this was not so is shown from Cohen's evidence alone, and of course there were other 'links.'

himself, must remain present. In Ernest's presence, then, the Swiss explained to "Archambault" the circumstance in which he had come to signal him to London as a traitor. Ernest recollected the words the Swiss said he had made his radio operator send, as: 'If "Archambault" is still transmitting he must be a traitor, for he is in German hands.' The Swiss wished to apologise to "Archambault" because, now that he too was a prisoner, and could appreciate the position, he realised that "Archambault" did not himself transmit the messages sent in his name; at the same time, being now himself a prisoner, he was unable to let London know that he had made a mistake. He had no means to retract the calumny, in the quarter where it mattered. The message he had caused his radio operator to send would have been received by their chiefs in London, and there was nothing he could do about it, except ask forgiveness.

"Archambault" had taken it philosophically. 'Don't worry,' he had said to the Swiss, so Ernest told me. 'You are certainly not the only one who has reported me to London as a traitor.' He had besought the Swiss in a kindly spirit not to have it on his mind, and declared, 'We shall be able to clear it all up when we get back to London after the war.'

Ernest regarded "Archambault" as an intrinsically sweet natured boy, and this was one of the episodes he recalled to prove it.

I had never doubted that this story was true; nevertheless, I was delighted to have it so unexpectedly confirmed from our own side of the fence, for Ernest had not been able to tell me the name of the radio operator who sent the messages for the Swiss Organiser.

Monday I went back to *France-Soir* to start a new week's search of their files.

Late on Wednesday afternoon at last, I found myself staring at a full-face photograph of *Le Capitaine*[24] *"Gilbert"* and a caption concerning his acquittal. The issue was dated June 8th, 1948 (the trial must have taken place on the 7th), and on enquiry at the sales desk I was told that an order for this date could be accepted.

As I came out, I saw the lights of *Parisien-Libéré* winking at me only a few yards further down the rue Réaumur. I had just time to get in there and turn up their issue for June 8th — their report was much longer than *France-Soir*, — before they closed. Now, it was only a matter of finding the addresses of the other newspaper offices and making the rounds. In the next couple of days, I got the reports from *Le Monde* and *Paris-Presse*, *Figaro*, *Franc-Tireur* and *Libération*, Whilst they all covered the same ground, almost every one carried some new detail and from the combined reports it was possible to gather a fairly full account of what had happened.

At 10 o'clock in the morning "Gilbert", aged thirty-eight, had appeared before the *Tribunal Militaire Permanent de Paris* in a court-room of the Reuilly Barracks, dressed in a dark blue suit with a discreet white stripe. More than one paper noted with approval that he had had the good taste to remove the *Légion d'Honneur* from his buttonhole. His gaze was direct and his personality commanded instant sympathy, said *Libération*.

When he went into the box the President of the Court, M. Dejean de la Batie, asked him whether he denied having been in contact with the Germans.

'Not at all,' he replied, and *Parisian Libéré* commented that his sincerity showed in his answer.

---

[24] In France, Air Force ranks have the same titles as Army. *Capitaine* would therefore correspond to Flight Lieutenant in English.

On June 2nd, 1943, he told the court, he had received a visit at his flat from two German pilots whom he had known at Le Bourget when on the Paris-Cologne run before the war. Now they were wearing Luftwaffe uniform, but were quite friendly and invited him to come out and take an aperitif with them. He in his turn suggested that they should go to the Café des Sports at the Porte Maillot. But when they went downstairs and got into the car that was waiting below, he found three Germans in civilian clothes already seated in it, one of whom he heard addressed as Doctor. At the Porte Maillot the car stopped and the two pilots got out and he was about to follow them when he found himself detained by the Doctor. The car drove on into the Bois de Boulogne and he felt himself a prisoner. The Doctor now told him that he knew his entire history; he knew that he had left France via Gibraltar in 1942 and gone to England and engaged in the R.A.F. from which he had passed into the "French Section"; he knew the names of his chiefs in London, the capacity in which he had been parachuted back into France and the nature of his present duties. 'He knew all my life,' "Gilbert" told the court. 'I did not know what to do. I am an airman, not a spy.'

'I could have you shot as a spy,' the Doctor had said to him. 'But you are intelligent and we hope you will work for us.'

'And what did you reply?' asked the President of the Court.

'I accepted, naturally,' he said. 'Not for money, as some newspapers have alleged. Not from fear of death; for a pilot, death is a natural, almost a classic thing. And not from fear of torture; I have seen it and I do not fear it. But because I wished to carry on my work and save the forty-eight agents of the Intelligence Service who depended on me.'

From now on he had contacts with Boemelburg and others and felt himself 'a prisoner at liberty.' He thought it best to 'feign to work for them in order to keep the contacts for future exploitation.' So as not to awaken their suspicion that he was playing them double he had given them the locations of eight airfields which he had chosen in Touraine, out of fourteen. 'The information which I gave them was of no consequence. I threw sand in their eyes. The eight airfields which I disclosed to them had not been formally accepted by London and I knew that no aircraft would land on them. The Resistance did not suffer.'

The President asked whether he had informed his chiefs in London that he was in relation with the Germans.

'I did not trust the discretion of the intermediaries,' he replied. Besides, he had not wished to inform London in case the leak should get back to German ears. 'I gave nothing to Boemelburg except promises,' he said. 'If I spoke to him of airfields, it was to fool him, not to inform him.'

'What a dangerous game!' exclaimed the President.

'The more my merit!' he retorted.

Major Guyon, *Commissaire du Gouvernement*, put it to him that he had been on the field to receive Majors Boddington and Agazarian when they landed on July 15th; that he had known that they were going to keep a rendezvous, as they thought, with Gilbert Norman ("Archambault"); that he had known that the latter was a prisoner in German hands and had failed to warn them.

"Gilbert" protested. 'Agazarian had a rendezvous with Norman in the rue de Rome. "Don't go there," I said. "He has been arrested. His concierge told me."'

Major Guyon: 'Did you say that it was from the Germans that you knew this?'

"Gilbert": 'It would have been no use. To convince a senior British officer that he is mistaken is impossible.'

The German witnesses, Colonel Dr. Knochen (Kieffer's chief), Dr. Goetz, Joseph Placke of Kieffer's department and Sergeant Bleicher of the *Abwehr*, seemed, when called into the box, to have had very little to say. Cross-examined by Maître Moro-Giafferi for the defence, they agreed that very likely "Gilbert" had only pretended to work for them, that he had in fact told them nothing of value, and that he interested them only in as much as they hoped he might one day be able to tell them the date and place of the invasion.

That closed the morning's session. When the hearing was resumed in the afternoon the whole ground was taken from under the prosecution when 'the very mysterious' Major Boddington described in nearly all the papers as 'of the Intelligence Service,' went into the box.

'"Gilbert" told me of his contacts with the Germans in July 1943 within a few hours of my arrival on the airfield at Candé,' he declared.

'And what did you say?' asked Maître Moro-Giafferi.

'I advised him not to break his contacts with the Germans. It was the natural thing.' He had remained in France until August 15th, or according to some of the reports 16th, a whole month, during which he saw "Gilbert" a number of times, and must have been arrested had "Gilbert", who knew his address, betrayed it. 'If I had to start all over again, I would start with "Gilbert",' he said.

It appeared that more than 240 people had passed from "Gilbert's" airfields and through "Gilbert's" hands to England and safety; among them General Zeller, who wished to shake his hand, General Ely,[25] Monsieur Mitter-and, *Minister des Anciens Combattants*, M. Roualt, director-adjutant of the *Prefect de Police*, M. Livry-Level, *deputé* for Calvados, Madame Felix

---

[25] Today Commander-in-Chief of the French Armed Forces.

Gouin, Madame Pierre Bloch, Major Gerson, M. Rachet, M. Didier Daurat and M. Wuyard who had belonged to "Gilbert's" own group. A succession of witnesses filed through the box, and those who could not come in person sent written testimonies.

Major Guyon, seeking to delay the acquittal he saw to be inevitable, asked the President to put some supplementary questions. Maître Moro-Giafferi, riding the tide of victory at the flood, would have none of it. 'If he is guilty of treason,' he cried, 'there is still death and the firing-squad for traitors. If he is innocent, give him back his honour.'

The *Juges* retired. They were out only two minutes. When they returned it was with a unanimous verdict for acquittal. There was applause in Court. "Gilbert" hurried out. He had to be recalled, for he had overlooked a formality. The *Commissaire du Gouvernement* had yet to read the verdict to him. Whilst he did so, six soldiers with fixed bayonets presented arms.

It was obvious that it had been a popular acquittal; "Gilbert" had captured the sympathy of most of the press and regret was expressed that he had been held in custody for an unusually long time before being brought to trial. 'Eighteen months is a long time in the life of a man,' said *Libération*. 'What can compensate the eighteen months spent in Fresnes and the calumnies showered on his head?'

For me, holding the statement I did from Ernest, these charitable expressions held a sad irony. It was, of course, Boddington's evidence which had been decisive; and presumably this was the British intervention to which the French referred. That "Gilbert" had refused Boddington's address to Kieffer, I knew from Bleicher's story; it was therefore to be expected that Boddington would witness for him. If he had passed through "Gilbert's" hands to safety, he was almost bound to come forward and say so. If "Gilbert" had, in fact, told him that he was in contact with the Germans, he was bound to say that, too. But what did he mean when he said that he had authorised him not to break his contacts with them? He was not sufficiently senior in the organisation of S.O.E. to give such sanction on his own authority except as a temporary measure, and would have had to report it immediately on his return to London. Was one to believe that the London headquarters had authorised "Gilbert" to maintain contact with the Germans, and at the same time to continue as Air Movements Officer for the "French Section" for the next six months, from Boddington's return in August 1943 until February 1944 when "Gilbert" was recalled?

Agents who had been arrested and who had escaped were, I knew, always held to be technically suspect, even if really trusted, because of the possibility that they *might* have been 'turned round'; and "Gilbert's" was a key position, as almost every agent arriving in the northern part of France passed through his hands. Not to betray them to the enemy, while maintaining contact with the enemy, over so long a period of time, even supposing his good faith, must place an almost impossible strain on his firmness and ingenuity.

I wondered whether Boddington had had to obtain a dispensation from the Official Secrets Act in order to give this evidence to the court, or whether he had perhaps been sent to give it.

It was, observed several of the newspapers, the weakness of the prosecution that it had not been able to point to a single person arrested through the agency of "Gilbert." But no mention had been made of his passing the mail to the Germans, and according to Ernest it was through this that the downfall of the whole "Prosper" network had been brought about. And according to Ernest, it was not unused airfields which he disclosed to them, but airfields that were being used.

All the papers spoke of both Boddington and "Gilbert" as belonging to the "French Section" of the Intelligence Service; this I took to be journalistic error, forgivable enough since the initials S.O.E. were virtually unknown in France and the French generally took the "French Section" to be a part of the Intelligence Service. But it seemed to me that here could lie the germs of more than a verbal confusion, in intelligence proper, where 'plants' and double-agents were the rule, a man might well be briefed to play the role of a traitor, in semblance only, in order to obtain information concerning the enemy's method of working; but S.O.E. was not concerned with intelligence. Its functions were sabotage, the reception and storage of arms, and the training of an underground army which should rise at the time of the invasion. Agents who sent back information about enemy movements were sometimes reminded that intelligence was not their job. If the court were perhaps no more clear than the press about this, the idea of "Gilbert's" being approved in his double-role by his chiefs in London would appear less strange than it did to me.

The question of dates perplexed me; Boddington said he had arrived on July 15th and that "Gilbert" had told him immediately of his contact with the Germans. If "Gilbert" had told him that this dated from June 2nd, Boddington had apparently not considered whether the arrest of "Prosper" and his colleagues on June 24th might not have derived from it. On the other hand, it seemed strange that "Gilbert" should have avowed that his contact with the Germans dated from before the disaster, if indeed he was telling a fairy-story. If he were going to lie, why had he not made a proper job of it and said that it happened after the 24th, or indeed only just a few days before Boddington arrived? Why avow June 2nd?

It occurred to me now that there ought to be reports not only of the acquittal but of the arrest of "Gilbert" eighteen months earlier.[26] On Saturday morning, therefore, I went back to *France-Soir* and recommenced from where I had left off before. In the issue for November, 29th,[27] 1946 I found it. DOUBLE AGENT CAPTAIN "GILBERT" ARRESTED.

---

[26] With regard to the length of time which can in France elapse between the charge and the trial, a word of explanation may not be amiss. In England it is not considered right that a charge should be made unless and until the grounds for making it have become pretty solid. In the French ethic, a person suspected of a crime is entitled to be informed officially at the *earliest possible moment* that he is suspected, what he is suspected of and why he is suspected of it, and so given a chance to explain, if he is able, the circumstances which have given rise to the suspicions. This is how it comes about that he is charged at a stage where he would in England be described, more likely, as 'helping the police in their enquiries.' The investigations continue afterwards, and are conducted, after the case has been passed from the Police, D.S.T. to the *Tribunal Militaiie* (in a service case), by an officer appointed to be the *Juge d'Instruction* of the accused. Since many witnesses may have to be discovered, called and heard, his task may be a long one. In many cases, the *Juge d'Instruction* accepts the word of the man he has to examine (there is no bail system) that he will hold himself available for questioning whenever required, and so he is able to carry on his life in the world; but this is a matter of discretion and in "Gilbert's" case it had not been exercised in his favour and he had spent the time in Fresnes prison. If the examinee satisfies the *Juge d'Instruction* that the suspicions entertained against him are groundless, or insufficiently substantial to warrant hearing before court, then the *Juge d'Instruction* discharges him on his own responsibility with a paper called a *Non Lieu*; if he feels, however, unable to sign a *Non Lieu*, he commits the case to trial before court.
[27] The actual date on which "Gilbert" was arrested was, as I learned later, November 26th.

On Monday I obtained the November reports from *Figaro*, *Le Monde*, *Parisien Libéré*, and of both numbers of another newspaper *Combat*, whose offices I spied going down the rue Montmartre in the evening. Here they were, I think, unused to people desiring to consult their back numbers for they had to get them out of nailed-up crates with the aid of a hammer; when eventually the whole pile fell out on the floor with the shavings, they sold me the two numbers I wanted for the small original price marked on them. Next day, Tuesday, I got the November reports from *Libération* and *Paris-Presse*, and both numbers from one last newspaper office, *L'Aurore*. Currency had all but run out and with these in hand I collected my case from my hotel, settled up and caught an evening flight bound for London. Seated in the aeroplane, I examined for the first time my precious papers.

From *Parisien Libéré* I learned that "Gilbert" had before the war flown for a commercial airline (on the Paris-Cologne run as I found elsewhere). At the same time, he had proved a brilliantly skilful pilot and had broken several world records for light aircraft. These exploits had opened to him the doors of Villacoublay (headquarters of the French Air Force) and the outbreak of war found him a test pilot. When, after the occupation, he went to England, it was therefore natural that he had gone into the R.A.F.

More than one of the November reports mentioned that after the war, at Easter 1946, "Gilbert" had been convicted at Croydon of smuggling gold and platinum, but let off with a light fine. *Combat* made the comment: "One may suppose that the Intelligence Service helped him out of it."

I decided that as soon as I got back to London I must try to find out about this affair at Croydon from the British end.

There was one other point of interest in the copy of *Combat*, upon which I meditated in the plane bearing me homewards. Following his recall from the field, it said, "Gilbert" had been arrested and held in custody in England for sixty days ending September 1st, 1944.

I knew from Ernest that "Gilbert" had gone back to England in February, 1944, in answer to the recall, and with the hopes of bluffing it out. What happened after he arrived in England, what questions he was asked and what story he told to allay the suspicions which had apparently formed there, there was no way to find out. Plainly enough, he had satisfied the British authorities, at any rate to the extent that they had released him without sending him for trial. I knew that agents returning from the field were sometimes held at a country house near Guildford while they made their reports and while these were being considered, and I knew also of one case where two such returning agents had been transferred from the house near Guildford to a cell in Brixton prison,[28] though no charge was preferred and they were eventually released. Presumably, something the same had happened to "Gilbert."

It is usual in France for the police, including the D.S.T., to issue a pretty full statement to the press of their reasons for making an arrest; this is without prejudice to the principle, as absolute there as here, that the accused must be presumed innocent unless and until proven guilty, and even though it licence the press to a degree that would here be considered contempt of court, is regarded as a safeguard against the advent of secret arrests on unknown charges such as can take place in totalitarian countries. Thus the newspapers announcing his arrest in Paris were able to proclaim that "Gilbert" was accused of having, during the period of his

---

[28] See *Inside North Pole* by Pieter Dourlein.

S.O.E. mission, entered into treasonable relations with Boemelburg, Goetz, Placke and with the "Bony-Lafont gang"[29] at the rue Lauriston; of having, in return for payments of some millions of francs, kept Boemelburg informed of the times when agents from London were to land on his airfields; in consequence of which the agents of Bony and Lafont followed them and arrested them a day or two later, generally as late as possible so that "Gilbert" and his fields should not fall under suspicion in London. *Combat* carried the detail that a German (unnamed) of the Avenue Foch had said: 'It was through Captain "Gilbert" that we achieved our greatest masterpieces of the war; he frequently received payments of several thousands of francs.'

This was in line with what Ernest had told me; yet these charges had not been brought up at his trial. What had happened? Had "Gilbert" been able to dispel them in the course of the preliminary examinations? They were apparently based on German evidence; yet the German witnesses in court had had practically nothing to say. Had they retracted their original statements? One at least must have done so. Or had the evidence been drawn less from the statements of living Germans in French hands than from captured documents? The newspapers declared that the information leading to the arrest was taken from captured German files; but Ernest was positive that in Kieffer's department at any rate they had left no files at the Avenue Foch and had, when they evacuated the premises, destroyed everything they did not take with them.

I was able to send Ernest copies of *France-Soir* and *Libération* bearing full and three-quarter face photographs of "Gilbert", and he replied saying that he recognised him. He thought the

---

[29] Bony and Lafont were two French Collaborationists of particularly infamous repute; both executed by the French in December 1944.

defence clever though he did not believe the story which
"Gilbert" had told the court. 'It was not solely in order to
know when and where the invasion would take place that we
maintained relations with "Gilbert" over such a long period of
time, and allowed him to work freely despite knowing of his
field at Angers.'

On the subject of Boddington and Agazarian, Ernest
confirmed what Cohen had told me. 'Our department knew of
Boddington's stay in Paris in 1943. Kieffer knew that he was
coming some days before his arrival in Paris. We offered him a
rendezvous at one of the letter-boxes in Paris controlled by
Kieffer. But instead of coming himself, Boddington sent his
radio operator [Agazarian] who had come with him from
London. While the radio operator went to keep the
rendezvous, Boddington remained in the neighbourhood of
the house in question to await the result. The radio operator
was arrested at this address and Boddington fled. It was the
radio operator himself who recounted all this to me while
being interrogated by me. He was not pleased with
Boddington.'

He concluded his letter, 'I cannot do otherwise than advise
you to be very prudent in anything that you publish concerning
the "Gilbert" affair. You may have enormous trouble.'
('*d'enormes ennuies.*')

CHAPTER FIVE: THE SMUGGLING CASE

The next thing was to find out whether there was anything in the English papers concerning the smuggling case at Croydon. So I went to the Newspaper Department of the Library of the British Museum, out at Hendon, and asked for the April 1946 volume of the two Croydon newspapers, *The Croydon Times* and *The Croydon Advertiser*. Here the case was big news. I also found afterwards a short paragraph in *The Daily Telegraph*.

Putting the accounts together, what emerged was this. "Gilbert," age thirty-six, a pilot for Air France, had brought an air liner in from Paris on the evening of 10th April, 1946, and was due to take off again at eight o'clock the next morning, April 11th. He passed through the Customs, but one of the Customs officers, happening to walk down the same passage, which led to the aircraft, five minutes before it was due to take off, noticed him closing up a bag. He asked "Gilbert" what it was he had put into it.

'A box of cigars,' said "Gilbert."

He therefore invited him to return to the Customs where he had previously shown a canvas bag and declared one pound of coffee, 200 cigarettes and a child's second-hand coat. When the briefcase was opened, it was found to contain, under a pair of pyjamas, fifteen pieces of platinum and one nugget of gold. The canvas bag was then searched. In it were 139 pieces of gold bullion, some in nuggets and some in strips, and £1,320 in £1 notes.

The platinum weighed 20-lb. 1-oz. and was valued at £3,158; the gold weighed 14-lb. 10-oz. and was valued at £1,500. The fines leviable were £9,474 on the platinum, £4,500 on the gold and £4,260 in the notes — a total of over £18,000. In addition, smuggling was punishable by imprisonment.

"Gilbert" also produced another £100 in £1 notes which, he explained, had been paid him for carrying the metal to France. Meanwhile, the aircraft was still waiting on the field for the pilot.

As "Gilbert" was the pilot he was, after some discussion, allowed to proceed to it, and to fly it back to France. "Gilbert" then, of his own accord, returned immediately to England in order to face the charges at Croydon.

He appeared the next day, April 12th, briefly, before the Magistrates at the Croydon Borough Court and was remanded in custody; on April 23rd he appeared again, and was defended by Mr. Derek Curtis Bennett, K.C., assisted by two Junior Counsel. "Gilbert" now told the Bench that he had, about two weeks before, met in Paris a man whom he had known in 1944 when they both belonged to S.O.E. and who bore the code-name "Ignace."

"Ignace" told him that he was now building up a new underground movement and needed funds, invited him to co-operate by bringing them over from England and, on his consenting, instructed him to contact a Mr. Robert Marshal at the Savoy Hotel in London and to give him a lady's white handkerchief. 'I was to give him the handkerchief so that he would know I was the right one,' explained "Gilbert." Having brought in his aircraft on the evening of the 10th, he telephoned Mr. Marshal at the hotel and a meeting was arranged. He gave Marshal the handkerchief as arranged and was, in return, handed a parcel which Marshal told him contained £10,000 worth of gold and platinum. It was the contents of this parcel which he had attempted to smuggle.

Mr. Curtis Bennett, defending, told the Bench that "Gilbert" had escaped from France in 1942 by way of Spain, that he had come to England and joined the R.A.F., and that in 1943 he had been parachuted back into France as an agent of S.O.E. for the purpose of carrying on underground activities. He had been sent on secret missions; he had been trusted and his word had been accepted. He was traced by the Gestapo, escaped to England and was parachuted into France for the second time in 1944, 'on important work for the underground in preparation for the invasion.' For that work he had been recommended for the D.S.O. and held the Croix de Guerre with three bars. Later, he had rejoined the Air Force, had been seriously wounded when his aircraft was shot down, and had spent some time in bed.

'I suppose that during his work in France he would think nothing of carrying two dozen fictitious passports,' said Mr. Curtis Bennett. 'He has spent most of his life doing unorthodox things, for which he has had credit.' The French Resistance movement was still in being 'to protect democracy should it again become necessary' and "Gilbert," who was still a member of it, was doing a job for it. As a result of his action, he had already lost his employment with Air France.

The Magistrates recognised that he had lost his career; they appreciated also that he had returned willingly to face the charges, and said that, while the offence was serious, they realised 'the seriousness of the defence.' They imposed (according to the newspapers) a fine of £300 on the charge connected with the platinum and £200[30] for attempting to take out of the country the gold and notes, and recommended the defendant for deportation.

---

[30] According to "Gilbert" himself, I was later to learn, the total amount he was required to pay was only £400.

"Gilbert" had thus got off with a very light fine in place of the possible £18,000! Doubtless the fact that "Gilbert", a French citizen, had of his own accord returned from France in order to face the charges had weighed with the Magistrates; they had said as much, and one could believe that it had not only surprised them but must have commanded their sympathy. But that his Counsel should have urged his war service struck me as ironic, holding as I did Ernest's testimony. One could suppose that "Gilbert's" Counsel was as ignorant as the Bench of the equivocal nature of these services, and the minor inexactitudes regarding the dates, etc., were without significance in the context. If "Gilbert" had rejoined the Air Force and been shot down this was presumably after his release from S.O.E. on September 1st, 1944, on completion of their enquiries. What did surprise me, however, was that nobody should have asked what kind of Resistance Movement could still have existed in France in 1946.

CHAPTER SIX: THE ABBÉ OF ARDON

On April 22nd I received out of the blue a large envelope covered with French stamps, the bulging contents of which proved remarkable. My correspondent was the Abbé Paul Guillaume, whom I remembered as Mr. Norman's enemy. He had been reading *Madeleine* in the French translation which had appeared some time previously (the letter came through my French publishers) and sent me some papers he thought would interest me.

They certainly did. They were extracts from testimonies which had been made to the D.S.T. by Placke, Bony and Lafont.

Placke's, made on April 1st, 1946 (I translate from the French), read:

> In May or June 1943, the German police (I do not know which branch) arrested in Paris or in the region of Blois the English Lieutenant BOB[31] STARR. He was brought to the Avenue Foch, where he was to remain until August 1944, date of his departure for Germany with Kieffer. I do not know whether Bob had been beaten; but in any case, he was entirely in accord with us; he aided our department powerfully in the transmission of messages to London. When Kieffer's operations required a radio contact with London on short waves we always called on Bob Starr who, aided by two specialists of the *Abwehr* attached to the Avenue Foch for coding,

---

[31] Correctly, Captain John Starr, "Bob" was his code-name.

composed the text. He had great experience, having been a specialist in England.

Bob stayed all the time at the Avenue Foch; a little room was reserved for him on the fourth floor; he took his meals with us and accompanied us outside. I myself went out with him three times; once in Paris to take him to eat in a restaurant, another time to Saint-Quentin with my mistress, Helen... This followed an intercepted radio message instructing us to look for the wreckage of two aircraft which had failed to return from a mission. Dr. Goetz had charged me to discover if they were the same aircraft which had been fired on by the antiaircraft batteries at Chauny and Arras, which in fact they were. The third time it was to take him to Soissons, again with Helen … I went there to intercede on the behalf of a woman who had been arrested with her children and whom a friend had asked me to help...

In June 1943 Kieffer called me into his office. There I found Dr. Goetz and Karl Holdorf, from the rue de Saussaies, who spoke English perfectly having been steward on an American boat. Kieffer explained to us that his department had arrested a radio operator of the Resistance and that in the course of a rendezvous with this latter an Anglo-Canadian Lieutenant, "Bertrand" (arrested June 21st at Dhuison with "Valentin" alias McAllister: "Bertrand's" real name was Pickersgill) was also arrested. He had been parachuted to undertake the organisation of a network in the North of France; after the interrogation of these two men, in which I did not take part... Kieffer's department, substituting itself for "Bertrand," entered into relations with London. London replied with instructions to make contact with M.

Despret at Hirson [Aisne]. In his message, "Bertrand" had declared, according to Kieffer, that he had missed a rendezvous with his radio-operator and could communicate with London thanks to another network. It was at this moment that Kieffer called me in. Holdorf and I were to go to Hirson, Holdorf as "Bertrand" and I as a friend from Paris. M. Despret was suspicious all the same, and said he did not want to get mixed up in anything, that he was watched by the S.D. in St. Quentin and that there had been arrests in the region. Because of his attitude we returned to Paris without having achieved anything. Kieffer, once again assuming the role of "Bertrand," and with the help of Bob Starr, sent a further message to London, and London replied with instructions to make contact with the cloakroom attendant in the basement of the Colisée and ask her for Mlle. "Madeleine."

This we did, Holdorf and I, and indeed a young English girl who told us her name was "Madeleine" was there waiting for us. Holdorf had a long conversation with her in English. We spoke of the contact in Hirson which had come to nothing; she thought it was "Bertrand" with whom she was speaking. We arranged to meet her again the next day at the Etoile; she was going to arrange for us to make contact with M. Despret through somebody else.

Next day, indeed, we met with her a man of about thirty-five, whose name I have forgotten, and he led us I think to 6 rue Cambacérès. In the office of the management of the foundry I met a M. Dagnaud and, once more, M. Despret and also M. Coupeau, director of the foundry at Cateau [Nord]; as soon as the introductions had been made he went off.

The aim of my department was the same as that of Lieut. "Bertrand," that is to maintain relations with London, to arrange for the reception of parachute cargoes in the North and to confiscate the containers received to the profit of Germany; and eventually to utilise the agents parachuted to the "Bertrand" network, sometimes on behalf of other networks. The meeting between myself, Holdorf and M. Despret at the rue Cambacérès must have been in August 1943.

After the first contact, M. Despret had more confidence in us; we agreed that he should form at Hirson a reception committee of four men under Hector. M. Coupeau suggested the same thing for Cateau; I introduced him to one of our agents, Louis Blanchard, former volunteer for the L.V.E., of Levallois, since killed in a car accident by the Louvres, and Camille Augier, who drove. I told M. Coupeau and Hector that I had a lot of work, as a pretext for handing them over to Louis Blanchard.

After that Blanchard, aided by Michel Bouillon, who was from Caudry in the North, organised the reception of parachute cargoes. The radio link with London continued all the time. We signalled the location of the fields, always in the name of "Bertrand"; parachute deliveries were made at St. Michel and at Cateau, as well as at Caudry [Nord] in May and June 1944. The exploitation of the French Section lasted into June 1944. There were also teams exploited by the S.D. at St. Quentin, always in the name of "Bertrand," as well as six or eight fields round the town. For that matter, all over occupied France, particularly in the region of Orleans, Chartres, Bordeaux, Angers, Rennes, Rouen, and after March 1944, Nancy, the S.D. carried out the same operations. From the point of view of radio communication, it was all centralised under Dr. Goetz, except for the Rennes region where a transmitter was installed.

For myself, with Hector of Cateau, with Soumillon of Cateau, and with a dealer from Caudry, I occupied myself with the reception of parachute cargoes. By June 1944 I had received about fifteen drops. By each one of them ten to fifteen containers came down, which were sent to Paris and stocked at Satory. Except for the S.D. of Nancy which sent what it received straight to Germany.

In all these sectors operations went marvellously; I visited mine every six weeks. The French agents who took part in these operations were the following ... It was only on the fields at Caudry, Hirson and Le Cateau that we used real Resistants. In the other sectors this work was carried out by French agents of the S.D.

Five or six times to my knowledge London parachuted agents to France. We could not receive them on the fields where there were real Resistants; so we chose, in conjunction with London, a field and an hour favourable, so that they could be captured by our French agents when they came down. As I never concerned myself with the fields where we used French agents, I never participated in the reception of an agent from London...

In the spring of 1944 an Anglo-Canadian "Leonard" was arrested by the S.D. at St. Quentin and taken in hand by Goetz; the work which he was to have carried out at Nancy was taken over by our department and there were parachute deliveries.

The result of the work of the S.D. was therefore quite brilliant. Kieffer needed reinforcements after February 1944; I was concerned only with parachute receptions arranged under the orders of Goetz.

In March or April when a drop was made near Cateau, with the Soumillon team, there was a conversation between the crew of the aircraft and ourselves by means of a radio-telephone controlled by an *Abwehr* man.

From Paris under the direction of Goetz the messages were sent in English by morse! each time they were given to Bob Starr who put them into a jargon he knew well.

… In July 1944 Berlin judged it preferable that we should drop the camouflage … We sent a last message to London as follows: 'We thank you for all the arms you have sent us. GESTAPO.' Dr. Goetz claimed that London sent the advice, 'to us, Gestapo, to continue the work towards the East, but not too near to Berlin because of the Russians.' Goetz had no reason to say that if it was not true.

… When the S.D. withdrew from the Avenue Foch to the East, the English Lieut. Bob Starr followed the movement.

Here was the most astonishing deposition. In the first moment of shock, I scarcely knew whether it was more important as it affected "Madeleine" or Starr.

To think first about "Madeleine," here was confirmation of a story I had been told long ago but never really believed. Whilst I was doing the research for *Madeleine* I had interviewed a man whom I called in my first two books "X," who had told me a story about such a meeting at the Café Colisée; but because it lacked support and I had found his witness unreliable in other respects, I had never used it. Now I studied again the many pages of notes I had taken during the interview he had given me in the presence of his lawyer in 1949. It was clearly enough the same story: he said that shortly after the return of Boddington to London, that is in the latter part of August 1943, "Madeleine" had told him she had received radio instructions from London to go to the Café Colisée on the Champs Elysées and make herself known to the cloakroom attendant in the basement; the cloakroom attendant would then present her to two Canadian agents of the "French Section," whom she was in her turn to introduce to him in order that he might discuss with them the arrangements to be made in respect of a new network to be founded in the Ardennes; she did as instructed. The first meeting was between "Madeleine" and the two "Canadians" alone. After it she told him that she had arranged with them a second meeting at which he, too, should be present. They had then met, all four, at a place outside, and had gone all four into a restaurant to discuss over a meal the measures to be taken. It was only on September 30th, when he went to a further meeting with the two "Canadians," by himself, and was arrested that he realised they were not Canadians but Germans.

To "Madeleine," herself, clearly there attached no blame. She had followed to the letter the instructions she had received from London, and was not to know that the two men who presented themselves at the Colisée were not the right ones. Holdorf, who had learned his English as a steward on board an American boat would probably speak it with a trans-Atlantic accent that would sound to her ears sufficiently Canadian, and

I remembered Ernest telling me that Placke's English was so good that he had been able to pass himself off as an Englishman or Canadian to a number of people. London, itself deceived by the messages sent by the Germans in the name of the Canadian "Bertrand" after they had captured him and his colleague, had played the intermediary; London had put "Madeleine" into contact with Holdorf and Placke. It was therefore in all innocence that she in her turn had put Placke and Holdorf into contact with the French people with whom she was working and so formed an unconscious link in the chain that led to the German control, by Placke on behalf of Kieffer's department, of the network in the North.

I had heard a great deal about this network in the North run by Placke, from Starr, and had written a good deal about it in *The Starr Affair*. Yet until now I had never connected this story with that of the Café Colisée and the Ardennes. Starr had always spoken of 'the North' or '*le Nord*'; but a look at the atlas showed me now that Ardennes was a *departement* of Northern France adjoining *Nord*. It was obvious now that the fatal meeting at the Colisée to discuss the Ardennes related in fact to the beginnings of Placke's long control in 'the North.' It had run undetected by London until June, 1944, when a gambit of Starr's had put an end to it.

There remained outstanding the question why, if the Germans had been in contact with "Madeleine" as early as August, 1943, they should, in October, have needed to pay a Frenchwoman a substantial sum of money for an address at which they might arrest her. But perhaps Placke and Holdorf, after meeting her a couple of times, had lost sight of her; that could happen if they were more excited about the affair in the North, since it was in pursuit of this that they had met her incidentally. She would nevertheless, from that date, have been badly compromised. Presumably whatever she had said to Placke and Holdorf concerning her own activities and those of her associates would have gone to amplify the files at the Avenue Foch. (According to what Madame Balachowsky[32] told me, Placke had some twenty years of experience in espionage behind him).

Equally troubling in a different way were the references to Starr. I knew from Ernest that Placke had made an adverse statement to the *British* authorities regarding Starr, a copy of which Ernest had been shown at Staumühle by a British N.C.O. who seemed to expect a similar one from himself; but this for the French, I recognised at once, was something much more deadly than the one Ernest had described to me from memory.

In the first, bewildered moment I was struck, not solely by the allegations of collaboration, but by the number of mistakes. Starr had not been arrested in May or June; he had been arrested on July 18th. He had not been arrested in Paris or in the region of Blois, but on the road between Dijon and Dole. He had worked in a totally different area, in and around Dijon. This deposition made him sound as if he had been a member of the "Prosper" network, for Blois was in the very heart of the "Prosper" network which stretched from Paris all the way down the Loire to its mouth. If anyone who read this took it that Starr belonged to the "Prosper" network, then the mistake as regards the date would become significant. "Prosper," "Archambault" and "Denise" having all been arrested on June 24th, any member of their network arrested prior to that date could be suspected of having betrayed them. And then it dawned on me, in horror, that the mistakes might not be

---

[32] An important member of the "Prosper" network, who came to know Placke to some extent.

unintentional. After all, there were other statements which could only be deliberate lies. Placke must have been aware that Starr was not a wireless operator. Four months after the arrest of Starr, on November 18th, 1943, Starr's radio operator, Lieut. John Cuthbert Young, alias "Gabriel,"[33] and courier, Miss Diana Rowden, alias "Pauline,"[34] had been arrested together as an indirect result of a radio playback over another circuit, and brought to the Avenue Foch where "Gabriel" was asked by Kieffer's staff to reveal the location of the place where he had hidden his radio set; he refused and Placke must have known that this circuit never came under German control. Furthermore, if Starr had been a radio operator himself, it would not have been necessary for his chiefs in London to send "Gabriel" out with him to assist him in this capacity; and one could be sure that Placke very well knew, as did all the men of the Avenue Foch, the composition of the "French Section" teams: 1, Organiser; 2, Radio operator; 3, Courier. Even more obviously, Placke very well knew that Starr had not moved with Kieffer's department in its retreat from Paris; he had been sent to a concentration camp. Placke had gone with the department, and knew that they took no prisoners with them in their retreat.[35] I realised, with a queer

---

[33] Shot on September 6th, 1944, at Mauthausen, together with "Archambault" and five other British.

[34] Executed by injection with Denise at Natzweiler on July 6th, 1944.

[35] Placke's deposition also made passing reference to an Englishman called Harold Cole who had one of the rooms on the top floor of 84 Avenue Foch and was in the employ of Kieffer. I asked both Starr and Ernest if they knew such a person and they both answered me independently that they did and that he came to Avenue Foch about July, 1944, say three weeks or so before the Germans packed up. Starr said he had light sandy hair. Ernest said he never knew the nature of the work Cole did for Kieffer but he understood that, although he was English, he had been in the service of German

and disagreeable feeling, that I was for the first time holding in my hands a specimen of a kind of thing I had often heard of: a deposition designed to frame somebody. Designed to frame Starr.

I came to those by Bony and Lafont.

That of Pierre Bony, dated September 10th, 1944, read:

There was at 84 Avenue Foch, on the fourth floor, a prisoner, an English Captain, who occupied an office. Devoted to the German cause, his role consisted in receiving the messages in morse from London and sending them. He deciphered the codes easily and was able to know the fields on to which agents were parachuted into France.

Endowed with a prodigious memory, he reproduced in pencil the physiognomies of the agents, English and French, whom he knew, so well that it was possible to identify at sight, from his drawing, the person sought.

Intelligence for a very long time before he was transferred to Kieffer's department. Cole, he said, *did* accompany them in their withdrawal into Germany. It could be therefore that Placke was confusing Starr with Cole. At the time I would have hesitated to publish this in case it should be defamatory of an individual still living, but recently there has appeared a book called *The Way Back*, the story of Patrick O'Leary by Vincent Brome, in which there is treated at length the treason of an Englishman (now dead) called Cole. The author calls him Paul Cole. Both Starr and Ernest give the name as Harold Cole, as does Placke, but from other details which have since come to my knowledge there can be no doubt that it is the same man, and so there seems no reason not to refer to the matter. There is one more queer point. At Culioli's trial, Culioli said that 'Lord Cole' was an alias of Prosper , whilst a witness maintained that Cole was an alias of Archambault In fact, he was a separate individual but here again may lie the germs of a significant confusion.

Henri Lafont's, also dated September 10th, 1944, ran:

> About two years ago (at the beginning of 1943) a Captain of an English service was arrested by Kieffer's department: I never knew his name. He was placed in an office of 84 Avenue Foch. He spoke very good German, French and English. He was a very good draughtsman, and he was capable of drawing the portrait of someone without having him before his eyes; it was sufficient for him to have seen him once.
>
> Voluntarily, he gave full information concerning the agents under his orders. I remember that once in my presence he gave Kieffer the possibility of arresting a score of persons. He gave their names, their addresses, made a plan of the locality where they might be found and drew a portrait of each of them which was a very good likeness.
>
> He listened in to the radio transmissions and translated them for Kieffer. He knew the codes employed and was endowed with a prodigious memory. I always saw him in this office: he was on the short side, 1 metre 65, maximum height, moderate thickness, medium fair, about thirty-five.

Starr was clearly enough indicated, though again the information was false. He did not speak German; he had no knowledge of code or cipher; he was in civil life a poster artist and the bit about the portraits could have been inspired by the sight of Starr at work on the portraits (of which I had written in *The Starr Affair*) of Kieffer, Ernest, Von Kapri and other Germans; but no artist in the world could have drawn portraits of persons not before him with such accuracy as to enable others to go out into the town and make arrests from comparison with the drawings.

I realised with a shiver that these documents must have been in French hands at the time of Starr's examination by the French authorities. I had not known what Starr had been up against. And yet, there was consolation in this realisation; it meant that these depositions must have been taken into consideration and discounted. Their falsity must have been recognised both by the D.S.T. and by Major Mercier, Starr's *Juge d'Instruction*.[36]

I read the text first, barely noticing the names of the writers. With a sudden start, now, I realised that they were, indeed, BONY and LAFONT; the very chiefs of the odious Bony-Lafont gang of the rue Lauristen, whom I knew had been executed before the end of 1944. Their testimonies, dated September 1944, must have been made during the preliminary examination which preceded their trial.

And then suddenly I noticed something else: in the top left-hand corner of both the Bony and Lafont depositions was written: *Dossier, "Gilbert"* ("Gilbert" file. More exactly, it was "Gilbert's" real name which was used). So these papers had been considered in relation to the "Gilbert" case. And in the "Gilbert" case, they would appear as evidence for the defence, since if Starr had played the traitor there would be less reason to suspect "Gilbert's" hand in the downfall of the "French Section" networks. What was more, the re-duplication of the phrase 'endowed with a prodigious memory,' suggested that their testimonies had been made in concert or derived from a

---

[36] Starr had been given a *Non Lieu* in June, 1950, after an *Instruction* lasting seven months. Major Mercier had accepted his word that he would hold himself available for questioning, so that he had been able to carry on with his ordinary life during this time.

common source, a quarter where there was concern to protect "Gilbert."

The covering letter from the Abbé himself was friendly to me, though he seemed to accept the truth of all that was alleged in the documents he enclosed. He wrote from a little place called Ardon par Olivet in the Loiret.

I spent the morning typing out copies of all the enclosures and sent Starr a complete set of the passages concerning him.

He sent me a calming reply saying, 'All this is not new to me.' In 1947 when he had returned to France he had run into one of his former colleagues who had told him quite casually that he had been up at the D.S.T. and 'They would like to see you some time.' So he had taken himself there. An *Inspecteur* had said there were some documents on which they would like his comments and had read him out the depositions of Placke, Bony and Lafont. (As a matter of fact, I remembered now that he had told me something about this a long time ago, only the more recent investigation of 1949-50 by the *Tribunal Militaire* had overshadowed it.) It had not been difficult to show their falsity. The *Inspecteur* had asked him if he had any ideas as to why these three men should make false testimony against him. Starr thought that, in Placke's case, there might be an element of spite, for he had been able to put an end to Placke's network in the north; also Placke had, on one occasion, been reduced to lying to Kieffer (to cover a slight neglect of duty) in Starr's presence, and the recollection might be galling. As regards Bony and Lafont, he had genuinely no idea why they should have deposed as they had; to the best of his knowledge, he had never set eyes on either of them. The *Inspecteur* had thanked him for calling in, and that was the last he had heard of it. Although the depositions had been read to him he had not, as far as he could remember, had them actually in his hands to study; at any rate, he had not noticed that they were marked *Dossier, "Gilbert."*

I wrote to the Abbé thanking him for his thought in sending me all these papers, which I had indeed found very interesting, and saying I would like to see him if he would be so kind as to receive me in Ardon par Olivet. Would he tell me where it was, as I could not find it on my big atlas?

Near Orleans, he told me in his reply; he would be pleased to see me.

The fact that the Abbé was Norman's enemy was to me the source of a certain embarrassment; Norman had seriously contemplated bringing an action for defamation against the Abbé in respect of his publications concerning "Archambault." I did not want to play false by either side, so I wrote to Mr. Norman telling him I was going to visit the Abbé Guillaume and to the Abbé warning him that I was already in contact with Mr. Norman.

I flew to Paris on May 12th; Starr met me at the Air Terminal with his secretary, Monette, and as there was no room at my usual hotel I found myself settled in a pile of rugs on the floor of Monette's bathroom.

On Sunday Yeo-Thomas called for me at Starr's office. It was the first time that Yeo-Thomas and Starr had met since their encounter whilst prisoners at the Avenue Foch, and Yeo-Thomas took the occasion of assuring Starr personally that he would give evidence for him if there was an enquiry in England. Yeo-Thomas also said that he had been warned at the Embassy, by a worried friend, that if he insisted on concerning himself with *The Starr Affair* he would find himself getting into trouble, as they had had orders to 'play it down.' He refused to allow his actions to be influenced.

The next day, Monday, May 16th, I took the train to Orleans. From the town the way by road led across the river Loire, and then over a flatfish country, with stretches of heath, with occasional marsh, sparse woods, mainly birch, and ponds.

The Abbé had papers ready laid out for me on his desk in little piles. The first lot, bound together under one cover, were entitled on the outside, *Témoignages Ennemis (Enemy Testimonies)*. Though none of them was complete, they consisted of substantial extracts from the depositions made before the D.S.T. by a number of notable personages. There were twenty-eight pages of Placke, over fifty of Bleicher, and rather less of Bony, Lafont and some others whose names I did not know. I could take them home with me, he said, to study at leisure, if I would promise to keep them safely and let him have them back some time. Placke, like Bleicher, had made his after being handed over to the French authorities by the British.

I could also have a typescript volume as thick as a book, entitled *Mémoires d'une Chatte*, a document of "almost inconceivable depravity", but which he thought might have some bearing on my researches. "La Chatte" had in 1941 been, with a Pole, co-chief of an intelligence network they started together and which worked to London, known as the *Interalliée*, after she and he had been arrested on November 18th of that year she had become Bleicher's mistress and betrayed into German hands not only the whole structure of the organisation she had worked so hard to build up but those who had given her their loyalty. The radio set on which La Chatte's messages to London were transmitted was also captured and the transmissions continued under German supervision; it was the false information now sent over the *Interalliée* radio which had been in part responsible for the three German warships, *Scharnhorst, Gneisenau* and *Prinz Eugen* being allowed on

February 11th, 1942, to escape up the Channel. La Chatte while at supervised liberty had meanwhile made contact in December with Pierre de Vomécourt, the first agent of the "French Section" to be parachuted from London (on May 11th, 1941); in his company, with German approval, she had on February 26th, 1942, travelled to London by boat; in London, contrary to German plan she found herself detained. But a certain number of the agents of the original *Interalliée* finding themselves in German hands, had continued operations on behalf of Bleicher and his chiefs in the *Abwehr*, which came, in the following year, to effect a very important penetration of the "French Section."

I knew most of this story from the two German books; but it was new to me that La Chatte had written her own memoirs while in Holloway Gaol, and I accepted the loan of the volume gladly. This was, the Abbé believed, the only copy in existence saving that now in the *Tribunal Militaire*.

The Abbé himself had worked with one of the indigenous French Resistance groups which eventually came to find themselves acting in liaison with or gathered up into the "Prosper" network. Since the war he had become Correspondant for the Loiret of the *Commission d'Histoire du 2ème Guerre Mondiale*, and he was the author of a number of books about the history of the locality and its participation in the underground war. Concerning the region in the Loire valley known as La Sologne, comprising the modern *departements* of Loiret, Loir et Cher and Cher, he could speak with pin-point precision, having travelled and re-travelled it in search of testimonies. But when he came to the "French Section" or even to the "Prosper" network, he could only treat of its organisation in so far as it impinged upon his district; he had therefore difficulty in estimating the relative importance of the officers (whether British or French) sent out from the headquarters in London, and key personages figured in his scheme with little more significance than subsidiary ones. Thus, though he knew a certain amount about "Gilbert", and attached some importance to him because of his duties with regards to the airfields, he did not see him as a figure of overriding importance who controlled the arrivals and departures by air not only for this region but for practically the whole of occupied France. He told me, however, that "Gilbert's" wife had been active on his behalf during the time that he was under *Instruction*, seeking out Resistants who had been in contact with him during the German occupation and who had *not* been arrested, and particularly people who had been flown to London in safety from his airfields. To all of them she presented a questionnaire drawn up by "Gilbert" in prison. One man thus approached wrote to the War Office in London asking advice. He had received a reply advising him not to give evidence at the trial of "Gilbert" as he was believed to be guilty. The Abbé held a signed testimony from this man, but regretted that he would not be able to show it to me without first obtaining his permission, and that he did not know where he was at the moment.

To me it seemed extraordinary that a British official department should presume the guilt of a person who had not yet been tried; the advice was also puzzling because it was not in line with the evidence given by Major Boddington.

The Abbé showed me a copy of the deposition which Ernest made for the French authorities in 1949 concerning "Gilbert." It was in substance the same as the statement he had given me except that he gave "Claude" as an additional alias for "Gilbert." In fact this is not an alias "Gilbert" is known to have borne.

For himself, the Abbé inclined to think that "Denise" at least must have been independently trailed since her apartment at 51 rue des Petites Ecuries was over a café frequented by French agents of the Avenue Foch. According to a deposition of the proprietor, two of these, Mario Bay and Michel Bouillon (both executed by the French after the war) appeared to watch her movements.

The woman who 'did' for Monsieur l'Abbé now produced dinner beginning with some excellent locally grown asparagus. The question of Norman had so far lain silent between us; it was only over the asparagus that the Abbé himself raised it with the words, 'I suppose Mr. Norman thinks very bad things about me?'

'Yes,' I said. 'It is after all rather natural.' Mr. Norman's son had died in a concentration camp and he felt that whatever had happened at the Avenue Foch, which perhaps no one would ever understand completely, charity should spare the names of the dead.

The Abbé said he had been threatened with legal proceedings by Mr. Suttill and Mr. Norman in respect of what he had written in his books concerning "Prosper" and "Archambault". The pact was in any case a matter of history, as were its consequences. As regards the motives which inspired its conclusion, he would agree that this must remain a matter of personal appreciation based upon the characters involved; perhaps out of consideration for my position as a friend of Mr. Norman, he did not press the subject.

The Abbé confirmed the story of the poison pill of which I had first learned from Mr. Norman's files, and agreed that it was "Archambault's" intervention which saved Culioli's life at that juncture.

To understand the pill episode it was necessary to go back to yet another feud at the very origins of the "Prosper" network and indeed to the days before "Prosper" and "Archambault" had arrived on the scene, and the "French Section" was represented in the Loire valley by one "Gaspard". "Gaspard", real name Flower, in civil life a *maître d'hôtel*, had served in the R.A.F. as a cook before being transferred to the "French Section" of S.O.E. and parachuted.

Pierre Culioli had begun the war as a soldier and been taken prisoner, and it was after he was invalided out of a P.O.W. camp on December 25th, 1940, that he began, on his return to his native land, to take upon himself activities in connection with the Resistance; some time in 1942 these brought him into contact with "Gaspard", now established at Tours.

Next, in July, 1942, "Jacqueline" (Mrs. Yvonne Rudellat, F.A.N.Y.), the first woman to be sent from London into enemy territory, landed by boat in the south of France and made her way, as instructed, to Tours where she was attached to "Gaspard"; this was not to prove a happy combination. On September 23rd, 1942, two more (F.A.N.Y.) women, Andrée Borrel alias "Denise" and Lise de Baissac, were expected to arrive by parachute from London, and the field for their reception was laid out by "Gaspard." The pilot of the plane, Wing-Commander Pickard, had, when he looked down, considered it too narrowly encompassed by trees and, fearing that if the two women dropped they might land in the branches and be hurt, returned with them to London. On the following night, the 24th, Culioli laid out the field and they were successfully discharged, being the first women to make an operational parachute jump. It was thus Culioli who met them when they came down; they had been told they would be met by "Gaspard" and asked for him, and nobody could tell them why he was not in attendance. Miss de Baissac now proceeded on her way to Poitiers, while young "Denise" remained to prepare the way for "Prosper", who arrived by parachute in October and whose courier she became.

From now on there was rivalry between Culioli and "Gaspard." On November 1st, 1942, "Archambault" arrived by parachute on a field near Tours which had again been laid out by Culioli; it was therefore to Culioli, who was there to meet him, that "Archambault" gave an envelope which he had been given in London and which was marked on the outside; 'For Gaspard.' Culioli passed this on to "Gaspard", unaware that it contained a lethal pill destined to poison himself, for which "Gaspard" had asked when denouncing him to London as a doubtful agent. "Gaspard", having got the pill, spoke about it to more than one person and finally to "Archambault." "Archambault" was horrified to learn the contents of the envelope he had brought, refused to help poison Culioli and advised reconsideration of the idea. 'If you distrust Culioli,' he said to "Gaspard", 'why don't you ask London to have a plane sent to fetch him? That way you will be rid of him, and they can question him there and take any action they think appropriate.'

"Prosper" however made his own appreciation of the situation which had developed; having heard everybody, he sent "Gaspard" back to London and kept Culioli, whom he confirmed as chief of the sector in Touraine, with "Jacqueline" who had already transferred her allegiance to him, to be his courier.

For a while Culioli continued to lay out the airfields, a job he had taken on himself, but he was not an airman and, as the amount of air traffic increased, it was apparently felt in London that the reception not only of parachuted agents and cargoes, but of descending aircraft, which called for a good deal of technical knowledge, should be the responsibility of a man who was himself a pilot and therefore knew a pilot's problems. Thus it was that in January 1943 "Gilbert" was parachuted out to take over duties as Air Movements Officer.

On June 18th, 1943, two Canadians, McAlister alias "Valentin," with Pickersgill alias "Bertrand," as his radio operator,[37] were parachuted in Sologne, they had to make their way to the North where they were to found a new network, and on the 21st Culioli, who was charged to take them as far as Paris, picked them up in his car together with the material they carried, which included two radio sets, six crystals and four personal messages of which one was marked "For Prosper" and two were marked "For Archambault." These personal messages were packed together with the crystals and everything was put in the car. "Jacqueline" came too, and they were all four in the Citroën when it was stopped at a check-point before the Mairie at Dhuison and they were all made to get out and go inside. "Jacqueline" and Culioli were 'passed' and allowed to get back into the car, but the French of the two Canadians was so poor that when they had to speak the Germans on duty realised they could not be Frenchmen, and alerted, made a move to detain the car itself. Culioli, seeing that the game was up, let his clutch in and put his foot down; the Germans jumped into another car and set off in pursuit. Just outside the village of Bracieux they began to overhaul the Citroën and opened fire; a detachment at the entrance to

---

[37] In *The White Rabbit*, Pickersgill is given the higher rank, that is Captain, whereas McAlister is put down as Lieutenant. Notwithstanding, it was certainly Pickersgill alias "Bertrand" who was the radio operator, and the radio operator would normally be second in command to the Organiser. I do not, therefore, know which was the senior of these two.

Bracieux also fired on the approaching car and smashed the windscreen. "Jacqueline" fell across the front seat badly wounded. Seeing that there was no hope, Culioli, hoping to commit suicide, deliberately drove the car at top speed into the wall of a house, from which it cannoned off into a meadow. He was thrown out and five Germans sprang on him; he struggled desperately and was shot through the leg. Then he and "Jacqueline" were taken back to the Mairie at Dhuison where the two Canadians, McAlister and Pickersgill were still held, a search of their persons having brought to light papers concealed under their clothes.

Culioli was now given a somewhat rough and ready first-aid treatment by a German nurse who had been hurried to the scene and then while he was still feeling very weak from loss of blood the Germans set out in front of him what they had found in the car, the two radio sets, six crystals and four personal messages now unpacked.

The radio belonging to the Canadians was, as we knew, worked back to London by the Germans from this time on. So it was that I learned the origin of the pseudo-Canadian network in the North which had run under German control for a year, the two luckless Canadians having been arrested only three days after their arrival in France and before they reached the North at all.[38] Only in June 1944 was its run

---

[38] While this has been in printing a new book has appeared by Maurice Buckmaster: *They Fought Alone*, published by Odhams Press. On p. 75 appears a map of France on which various areas are marked off as those in which his agents worked. Against a large area on the North-Eastern border is given the name: Pickersgill. As will have been seen from the above account, Pickersgill never worked in this area or even reached it. He and McAlister were parachuted on June 18th and arrested on June 21st; the supposed 'Pickersgill' area was the German controlled one run by Placke under Kieffer's direction. (See Placke's long deposition cited above.)

brought to an end by Starr's manoeuvre with regard to the 'S. phone.'

Culioli was taken for interrogation first to Blois and afterwards to the Avenue Foch where he was shown the photostats of the "Prosper" mail. Here he was told that "Prosper" and "Archambault" had been arrested and of the pact which they had concluded with their captors, and invited to subscribe to it by disclosing the premises used for storage of arms within his area. He asked if he might speak with "Prosper" before giving an answer; and was told that it was not possible, but that he might speak with "Archambault." "Archambault" was then brought into the room in handcuffs. 'It is true,' "Archambault" told him simply.

Then Culioli, too, fell in with the terms of the pact to the extent of giving the names and addresses of four householders in the Sologne district, Couffrant, Gatignon, Le Meur and Cordelet, members of his own sector of the "Prosper" network, on whose premises the arms allotted to his groups were stored. To each of them he wrote letters in his own hand, explaining the position, expressing his regret that he was obliged to expose them, and asking them to hand over peacefully the arms in their custody. These letters he gave to the Germans to present when they arrived. All four

---

This map also reduces the "Prosper" network to a small area around Paris, though in his earlier book, *Specially Employed*, Lt.-Col. Buckmaster accords it a considerably larger extent and in fact we know that there were important sectors as far away as Le Mans (where Lieut. Garry was responsible), Poitiers (where Lise de Baissac was working), Tours and the Loire Valley as we have seen as well as at Gisors in the Eure (H.Q. of Captain Darling). There was also a Captain Wilkinson, alias "Alexandre," who, until his arrest in March or April, 1943, had had the charge of a network in South Brittany based on Angers founded in the first place by "Prosper".

householders were arrested; Couffrant, Gatignon and Le Meur survived.

"Jacqueline" never recovered from her wounds and, after passing through a chain of hospitals, was sent eventually to Ravensbrück and then in 1945 to Belsen where she was presumed to have died.

Pickersgill and McAlister were both hanged at Buchenwald September 9th, 1944.

Culioli was, in 1944, sent to Buchenwald, but survived.

In August 1945 Culioli was arrested by the French justice. Lequeux, now released and pardoned in respect of the information he had given following his own capture on July 18th, came forward to give evidence for the prosecution. He pointed out that Culioli had been captured three days before "Prosper" and "Archambault" and deduced therefrom that he must have betrayed both them and others. Here the Abbé remarked in parenthesis that "Prospers" own trust in Culioli had been such that he had asked for Culioli to receive him when he returned from London on June 20th although this should have been "Gilbert's" function as official Air Movements Officer. Culioli denied vigorously having betrayed either "Prosper" or "Archambault" but he declared having, in conformity with the pact, given the names of the four householders responsible for the stores of arms. During the preliminary examination a paper was delivered to the *Juge d'Instruction*, signed in the names of thirty-three members of Culioli's sector, expressing their confidence in his integrity and their readiness to give evidence for the defence. Amongst the signatories were the names of Couffrant,[39] Gatignon and

---

[39] Couffrant had earlier been charged with having in his turn given further information to the Germans after his arrest, but he had been granted a *Non Lieu*.

Madame Cordelet, the widow of the only one of the four householders who had died in Germany.

On the day of the trial, June 9th, 1948, "Gaspard" went into the box to say that he had distrusted Gulioli as far back at 1942, and distracted the court with the story of the poison pill which he would have administered to the accused but for "Archambault's" dissuasion. But the bulk of the evidence for the prosecution came from Lequeux and also from a female double-agent. The court found Culioli: 1, not guilty of intelligence with the enemy; 2, guilty of acts prejudicial to the national defence; he was pardoned without imposition of sentence.

In defiance of his advocate's advice to leave well alone, since he was now free, Culioli, insisting upon a point of honour, filed a petition for complete retrial before a higher court, and with good result. At Metz, on March 17th, 1949, he was found 'Not Guilty.'

Much of this I knew from the old newspapers on Mr. Norman's files, but told in the deepening shadows with the flickering gaslight illuminating the features of one who had, through all that had passed, remained devoted to Culioli, it took on all the drama of such a case of conscience.

I found my way up the stair with a candle to the room which had been prepared for me.

In the morning I packed into my suitcase the bound volume of *Témoignages Ennemis*, the *Mémoires d'une Chatte* and three of the Abbé's own books, including the most important from my point of view, *La Sologne au Temps de l'Héroisme et de la Trahison*, and caught the bus back to Orleans. Here, still clutching my suitcase which, if it had grown rather heavy, had grown also too precious to leave in the *consigne*, I took time off to make my way to the Cathedral and thence to the little statue of Joan of

Arc I had always wanted to see, and which I found surrounded by flowers. Then I caught the train back to Paris; and Monette's bathroom.

CHAPTER SEVEN: A LINK BETWEEN TWO THEATRES

Next day, Wednesday, May 18th, I felt that my first call should be on Mr. Norman, though there was not much new that I could tell him regarding his son.

Then, at six o'clock, I met Madame Balachowsky[40] for tea at the Café Murat by the Porte d'Auteuil. I tried to draw her on the subject of "Gilbert," but she would say nothing except 'We didn't know him.' Did I think it right to embarrass the authorities of my own country by making these enquiries?

She did, however, confirm what she had told me several years ago, that "Prosper" had returned from his brief visit to London, in June 1943, in a very strange state of mind. She put it, if anything, even a little more strongly than at our first meeting. He had returned believing that all their movements and all their operations were known to the Germans and probably had been known some time. He told her this on June 20th, the day of his return from a short visit to London, four days before his arrest. She had met him in Paris and he had come with her to the Gare Montparnasse to see her on to her train for Viroflay. This conversation had taken place on the steps of the Gare Montparnasse. He had not been in such a state of mind when he left for London ten days previously on June 10th. It was during those ten days in London that this dread conviction had come upon him.

'Did he say what had given it to him?' I asked. 'Was it something that he had seen or heard there?'

---

[40] One of the important members of the "Prosper" network.

She could not say. Presumably he had not disclosed his suspicions to anyone in London. He was convinced of a leak but could not put his finger on the place. He seemed to think it came *from* London. Now, though he had returned to rejoin his comrades who trusted him, he feared that the blow might fall any minute.

All this she had told me before, but so long ago that it was good to hear her repeat the facts (sombre as they were) in almost the same words she had first used.

The next day, May 19th, on an impulse, I called on Madame Aigrain, a member of the "Prosper" network with whom "Madeleine" had stayed for some time. I had not seen her since January 1950 when I was in the early stages of my research on "Madeline." Now I asked her — without much hope that she would have anything to tell me — whether she knew who had betrayed the "Prosper" network.

"'Gilbert,'" she said, without a second's hesitation.

"'Gilbert' who?' I asked, to be sure she was not speaking of Gilbert Norman alias "Archambault."

She pronounced the real name of "Gilbert," the Air Movements Officer.

Her evidence was circumstantial, but telling. She never met "Gilbert," but was accustomed to hear "Madeleine" refer to him, from time to time. On one occasion, a colleague of hers, Monsieur Andrès, had given her a sheet of paper bearing a communication for London, with the request that she pass it to "Madeleine" and ask "Madeleine" to send it by radio. "Madeleine" had taken it, but when she came back later she said that as it was a little long for transmission by radio and as there was an aircraft leaving, she had given it to "Gilbert" to put aboard. Madame Aigrain could not tell me the date of the report, but remembered that it concerned the results of an

R.A.F. raid on Boulogne-sur-Seine and Courbevoie, which had taken place about the middle of September. Later, after she herself was arrested, she was shown a photostat of this report at the Avenue Foch. The interrogator who had shown her this was, she believed, Ernest, though she would not affirm it in case she should be mistaken. He asked her for a specimen of her own handwriting (which she deformed as much as possible) as he wished to compare it with that of the report. He had been perfectly 'correct' with her, but there had been a moment of tension when he had asked her to sign something written in German, of which he gave her only a verbal translation; this she had refused to do, in case it really said something different from what he told her. 'You don't trust me?' he had asked. 'No!' she had replied, 'you are the enemy!' In the end it was he who had given way, saying that if she did not wish to sign it, it did not matter.

After the war, she had been called to give evidence at the *Instruction* of "Gilbert," and had told the *Juge d'Instruction* what she had told me. "Gilbert" himself had been present and it was then she saw him for the first and only time. He had protested against the implication inherent in the story, and denied that he had ever had contact with the Germans. 'I cannot speak a single word of German!' he declared. 'How could I have talked with Germans when I cannot speak German?'

As I left Madame Aigrain's, I reflected that poor "Madeleine" seemed to have been surrounded by Germans and German agents on all sides. Not only had she been in contact with Placke and Holdorf, but also with "Gilbert," who could have betrayed her at any moment to the German departments to which he submitted the mail. That he had not done so, at any rate in the sense that he had not been the instrument of her arrest, was a fact that had to be recognised, perhaps to his credit. I remembered Ernest telling me, when first I met him, that he was able to show "Madeleine" photostats not only of the "Prosper" mail but of a report she herself had written for her chiefs in London, and of a personal letter to her mother, the original of which had, like the report, been sent on its way. I had put this in my book *Madeleine*, though I did not then understand how it had happened and had never heard the name of "Gilbert." One could perhaps say that he betrayed the mail she confided to him, but had not betrayed her.

The chief importance of Madame Aigrain's statement seemed to lie in that it showed "Gilbert" as having continued to hand over the mail after his conversation with Boddington in July, of which Boddington had told the court at his trial; also after Boddington had authorised his maintenance of contact with the enemy — it looked as though Boddington had only known the half of it — and after Boddington's departure for London by the August moon. "Madeleine's" letter to her mother was undated, but it seemed probable that it and the report had gone back by the same plane (or rather, planes, for two left from the same field) as took Boddington, "Antoine," Lise de Baissac, her brother, Claude de Baissac, and some others.

That afternoon brought a surprise letter from New York from a Mr. Girard alias "Carte." He was the chief of the French network in the South of France to whom Starr had been attached when sent out on his first mission in August 1942. He had read *No. 13 Bob* (the American edition of *The Starr Affair*) and had been overjoyed to discover that it was about Starr, for whom he cherished a vivid affection and regard. He expressed the greatest support for the arguments put forward in the book and asked me to assure Starr how good was the memory he held of him. I was able to show Starr the letter.

I had brought back from me from Ardon such a mass of reading matter that I scarcely knew where to start on it. Placke's consisted largely of paragraphs dealing, one after another, with various Allied nationals concerning whom, presumably, he had been asked. There was one really exasperating feature. When he came to "Gilbert" he had written simply *"Gilbert" parlé ailleurs.* ("Gilbert": I have spoken elsewhere.) But if in fact he had, the 'elsewhere' did not figure in the volume. For the rest, the Abbé had really gutted it in the extracts he had sent me already.

There was, however, a certain amount more in the Bony and Lafont depositions. Both listed a series of occasions on which they had supplied teams, ranging from four to ten men, to go down to Angers on nights when Allied agents were due to be parachuted. Bony and Lafont had received their instructions sometimes from a Dr. Kuhn and sometimes from Boemelburg, but they believed that the operations were on Kieffer's behalf. They, who were directly responsible to Boemelburg, were not permitted to keep in their own custody any of the prisoners resulting from these particular operations. The job of the men they supplied was to accompany the arriving British agents on the train from Angers to Paris, where they would sometimes be arrested by a take-over team, sometimes merely followed further, in order that their destination and contacts might be noted. They did not give the dates of any of these operations or the names of any of the British agents met; they did declare that on one occasion the arriving party consisted of eight men and that these were all arrested as soon as they reached Paris, and that on another a party, which was merely followed, included a woman; this party split on arrival and two of its members called at the Café des Sports at the Porte Maillot.

The name of "Gilbert" did not appear; but Angers was his field. In view of what Ernest had told me, these depositions had a sinister implication. At the same time, bearing in mind the extent to which passages concerning Starr were fictionalised, I could scarcely accord an unqualified credence to any part of them.

Substantial portions of both the Placke and the Bony and Lafont depositions, including the passages alleging that Starr had worked for the Germans, appeared in the Abbé's book, *La Sologne*, together with his own speculations on the matter concerning Starr:

> 'At first sight, one is tempted to doubt the existence of this British officer, known only through the witness of the enemy …. But the three portraits are concordant, and it is difficult in the circumstances to doubt either the existence or the role of "Bob Starr," despite the silence of the English on the subject of this personage.'

I had enlightened the Abbé somewhat on my visit to Ardon; now, seeing how much he had printed in his book, I showed the pages in question to Starr and suggested that he should do something about it. 'Tell him I'll come and see him some time,' he said unemotionally. He was past becoming excited. I wrote to the Abbé saying Starr did not bear him any malice as he realised that he had published all this matter in good faith, but suggested that a correction might be inserted in any future editions, and that he would like to come and see him; in return I received a very cordial letter expressing the hope that Starr would indeed come down to Ardon and have lunch with him one day. (Somewhat later Starr did so, and I heard from both sides that the meeting was friendly; the Abbé submitted to Starr a copy of a statement he was sending to the *Commission d'Histoire du 2ème Guerre Mondiale* rectifying the information he had previously sent them, and also presented Starr with an autographed copy of the book!)

There was not a great deal from the point of view of my research in the *Mémoires d'une Chatte*, but, as a human document, it provided me with a good many evenings' bedtime reading, curled in my rugs on the tiled floor of Monette's bathroom.

Realising my interest in "Gilbert," the Abbé who was now becoming, as he was to remain, my faithful correspondent, sent me copies of three extracts from the depositions made by him at different times for the D.S.T. (the only fragments by "Gilbert" himself that he possessed.) One stated simply that he had been witness to the report made by Wing-Commander Pickard, D.S.O., D.F.C.,[41] in September 1942 on his return to London after an unsuccessful attempt to parachute containers and agents; it set out in technical language the reasons why Pickard had considered it would be dangerous to drop them, and was probably straightforward enough, since this subject would not have concerned "Gilbert's" own position. What I was interested to discover from it was that "Gilbert" had been at this date (prior to his transfer to S.O.E.) a Flight-Lieutenant in Pickard's Special Squadron: this filled in for me another chapter of "Gilbert's" own career.

One of the extracts was much more sombre in that it referred to "Prosper" and "Archambault" as having worked for the Germans after their capture. It cited the mysterious statement said to have been made by Winston Churchill in

---

[41] Later Group-Captain Pickard, the hero of the bombing of Amiens prison to release the inmates.

1943 in 'secret session of the House of Lords' (sic) that the invasion of the continent had had to be put back a year as the result of the 'treason of a Mr. X.' "Gilbert" affirmed that 'incontestably, he referred to "Prosper."' He had, he declared, been told of this speech of Mr. Churchill on his return to London in February 1944. He added that the two Canadians, Pickersgill and McAlister, were also 'suspect in London.'

In the other extract, "Gilbert" said that he had first learned of the arrest of "Prosper" from "Antoine"[42] at 9 a.m. June 24th, 1943, by the terrace of the Hotel Terminus at the Gare St. Lazare; he understood from "Antoine" that the arrest had just occurred in the nearby Café Dupont. Turning to the Abbé's book, however, I saw that the arrest of "Prosper" was stated to have taken place in an hotel in the rue Mazagran at 10 a.m. of the morning in question and the deposition of the proprietress, Madame Fèvre, was quoted in support. "Antoine" had been executed in Germany, so it was impossible to check with him.

I was all this time ploughing steadily through the mass of papers the Abbé had given me, not knowing where I should look first for the matters of greatest importance. It was only on Friday, May 27th, that I came on a deposition in the name of Christmann (as a matter of fact, I think this had been missing from the bound volume and the Abbé sent it to me afterwards, separately). Christmann was a new name to me, but it appeared that he was a Major of the *Abwehr*. The story and the matters which it set out were far from plain, even on reading with the greatest attention. The author was described as of the *Lutetia*

---

[42] One of the major agents of the "French Section" whose story weaves in and out of the "Prosper" network. See *Madeleine* and *The Starr Affair*.

(the H.Q. of the *Abwehr* in Paris), but according to the narrative he appeared to emanate from Holland. He was also described as the Chief of the *Nordpol* circuit; but, I knew, of course, it was Lt.-Col. Giskes who had been at the head of all *Abwehr* operations in Holland and specifically of *Nordpol.*

'It was towards the end of May 1943, that Colonel Blunt of the Dutch Section in London informed us that it was essential that we should get into touch with the "French Section" in Paris, it ran, '…. our network was registered in London and I myself was specially entrusted with the duty of arranging for the withdrawal of English and Dutch agents parachuted to us. Towards the end of May then, London insisted that we should send back the head of our sabotage network known by the name of "Anton." "Anton" was regarded in London as a very valuable man. It was agreed that the French Section should take charge of him in Paris and be responsible for his journey on. I myself was to play the role of "Arnaud," the Belgian head of the *Nordpol* circuit, and an adjutant of the *Abwehr* was to play the part of "Anton." London gave us the password which would enable us to meet "Gilbert" of the French Section who would take charge of "Anton." The meeting was to take place in a lodging on the third floor of a house 6 or 8 rue de Clignancourt [this should read 1 o Square Clignancourt] and the son of the tenant, Alain, was to act as the intermediary. Everything in Paris went according to plan except that instead of our making contact with "Gilbert," Alain put us by mistake into touch with "Gilbert-Archambault." Several meetings were necessary to clear up this misunderstanding, but in the end one Marcel, of the "French Section", took charge of "Anton." After the last meeting between Marcel, Alain, "Anton" and me, "Anton" alone was arrested by the S.D. at the Restaurant Capucines, so that he would not have to go to London.

'During the different meetings between ourselves and different members of the "French Section" we were always encircled by a security cordon provided by the S.D. They had orders not to arrest anybody lest it should cause our *Nordpol* operation in the Netherlands to be suspected in London. All this activity in Paris must have lasted until the end of June. In consequence of the surveillance established by the S.D., Section 4 E Untersturmführer Gutgessell sinned through excess of zeal and arrested Gilbert-Archambault and Alain. These arrests caused us a lot of trouble, and we were only able in *extremis* to prevent others, notably "Marcel" and "Denise" [in fact "Denise" *was* arrested together with "Archambault"] from being arrested too.'

It took me quite a long time to make sense of this narrative. It related, of course, to the time when the "Dutch Section" of S.O.E. was, unknown to London, under German control. That was why Christmann and his colleagues would have been receiving messages from London. The people in London, thinking they were still communicating with their own agents, had apparently asked for one of them to come back. As he would have been in a German prison, like all the rest, it must obviously have been impossible for the Germans to send him; but they had feigned compliance with the instructions and sent off one of their own men, accompanied for inexplicable reasons by Christmann, to meet the contact in Paris. Why had he had to go to Paris? Presumably, because London had not organised a pick-up air service for fetching agents back from Holland, such as they had for France; that was why the returning agent had to go to Paris to meet "Gilbert," the Air Movements Officer for France. The gesture made, the 'arrest' of the bogus Dutchman (in fact, a German) would be staged, so that he should not in fact have to go to England and so that the "French Section" agents should report a mishap.

Here, then, for the first time, was a link between the two theatres of Holland and France, between the German controlled "Dutch Section" and the German penetration of the "French Section." I felt that this was a matter of major importance. The disasters which had occurred in these two theatres had always been considered separately; was it now possible that what had happened in France was contingent upon what had already happened in Holland? Had the "French Section" been penetrated through, and as a consequence of, the German control of the "Dutch Section"?

I wondered at what level in London the decision had been taken to put the two national Sections into contact with one another. That such a decision had been taken suggested that in the top office of S.O.E. they must have felt extremely sure of the health of both the "French" and "Dutch Sections"; if there existed the slightest suspicion that either might have been penetrated by German agents, then to put that one into contact with its neighbour was to expose that neighbour to the infection. In fact, since it was the "Dutch Section" which had come to be completely German controlled, it was from Holland that the infection was led into France; notwithstanding that the Germans services in France had already made certain inroads on the "French Section."

It was in any case plain that "Archambault" had at this date, 'towards the end of May,' and in all innocence, been put into contact with the enemy by London. It was following radio instructions from London that he went to the Square Clignancourt to keep a rendezvous with Christmann and "Anton," even as later in the summer "Madeleine" went on instructions from London to the Café Colisée to meet Placke and Holdorf.

In his book *La Sologne*, where I found part of Christmann's deposition reproduced, the Abbé identified "Alain" as Alain Bussoz (executed by the Germans) and "Marcel" as Marcel Charbonnier of Pontoise, personal liaison agent to "Prosper"; from elsewhere I learned later that he worked particularly in the Gisors sector of the "Prosper" network. Though I never succeeded in tracing him (or at least received no reply from the address the Abbé gave me) he survived[43] to depose to the French authorities: 'Well before his arrest, "Prosper" was uneasy concerning the security of his network; I definitely remember his saying: "There are hard blows in prospect and it is from London that it is coming."' In *La Sologne* the Abbé added that in the course of a subsequent separate meeting between "Archambault", Marcel Charbonnier and "Anton" in the Pigalle district "Archambault" had given a radio set to "Anton;" though no partisan of "Archambault," the Abbé had made the observation that no reproach could be made against him for having done this since he had no reason to suspect that the pretended Dutchman "Anton" was a German. It was nevertheless a detail with most alarming implications. I could imagine that a misunderstanding of what had happened might give rise to rumours reflecting adversely on "Archambault," especially on top of the unfortunate coincidence that his Christian name was Gilbert.

Then there was the mystery of the confusion of names which had led to "Archambault's" turning up at the Square Clignancourt instead of "Gilbert"; at what level had the confusion taken place? Had "Archambault" received the message on his own radio, or had it been transmitted to

---

[43] It appears that in fact he was never arrested.

"Gilbert's" operator or some other, who had passed it to "Archambault" instead of "Gilbert"? There seemed to be a whole nest of mysteries hidden here. In any case, what about "Gilbert," "Gilbert" whom the travellers from Holland were expected to meet?

Could it be possible that Christmann had been in fact the first German to contact "Gilbert"? True, he did not actually say in his deposition that he had in the end contacted him; it tailed off in an inconclusive manner. Yet the man Christmann had been intended to meet was, obviously, "Gilbert" the Air Movements Officer; was it to be supposed that having discovered he had met the wrong man he would leave it at that and not attempt to find the right one? It seemed to me that the story had been left unfinished, perhaps purposely; surely it could have been made plainer if the writer had wished to make himself plain; but one had to remember that he was a German, and a prisoner, and that probably he didn't. If he had, in fact, gone on afterwards to meet the real "Gilbert" and had won him over to becoming a German agent, he might well feel that in making a deposition to the French he should conceal this and word it in such a way as to give him a little cover.

If "Gilbert" had, in fact, been contacted by Christmann, then he would, like "Archambault" (and later "Madeleine") have been put into contact with the enemy by London. If taxed, on his eventual recall to London, with being in contact with the Germans, he could truthfully have retorted: 'Who put me into contact with them? You!' Moreover, would this not have been the normal, and not altogether ineffective, defence he might have been expected to offer at his trial in France: he had been exposed to temptation when put into contact with an officer of the *Abwehr* by an order from London. If he had told this to the court, he would have been invited to explain the circumstances in which such a thing had happened, and the whole story of "Operation North Pole" would have been blown to the world from the courtroom of the Reuilly Barracks, through the medium of the press, in June 1948, instead of remaining unknown, outside the limited circle of those concerned, until the publication of Colonel Giskes' book *London Calling North Pole* in 1953. Had Colonel Giskes not written this book, the appearance of which was probably never expected and had the effect of an exploding bombshell, the story might never have become known to the British public. If "Gilbert" had had it in his power to explode the bomb in his own defence five years earlier, when on trial for his life, why had he not done so? Could it be that when he had been interrogated in London on his recall from the field in 1944, and such questions had been examined, an appeal had been made to him not to disclose the fact that the "French Section" had been penetrated through the German control in Holland?

I felt that I must find Christmann. I had done all I could in Paris; besides I had to be careful of currency. While a small legacy left me recently had, in conjunction with the royalties from my books, given me a modest independence and my time was my own, the currency regulations prevented my feeling the greater ease whilst on the continent. If I were to follow the trail of Christmann to Germany, and still to keep within my basic £100, then I could not linger in Paris.

I did stay a little longer, in the endeavour to trace some of the other persons mentioned in these depositions and in the Abbé's book, but was unable and decided that at least I should try to obtain a written statement from Madame Aigrain before I returned. She gave me an appointment and in my presence wrote me a letter:

June 9th

Mademoiselle,

I remember very clearly that in November 1943, in the course of my second interrogation at the Avenue Foch, the German who interrogated me showed me a photostat of a report made by one of my friends, Monsieur Andrès, since deceased.

This report was given to Madeleine after the bombardment of Boulogne and Courbevoie, and Madeleine told us that she gave it to Gilbert.

It is unfortunately impossible for me to be sure of the date.

Assuring you of my best wishes,

G. Aigrain

With that in my luggage, as well as all the other papers, I left Paris in the afternoon of the same day.

CHAPTER EIGHT: MYSTERY TOUR

My next task was to find Christmann, and I decided to write to a former Colonel of the *Abwehr*, whose name I had obtained from a book, addressing my letter care of the publishers of the book in question. I composed the letter with considerable care, explaining myself to the length of about four pages of type. The Colonel was under no obligation to answer my enquiry, and if I hoped for an answer I must arouse his interest and sympathy. I stated in so many words that I did not belong, and never had belonged, either to the Intelligence Service or to S.O.E. or to anything analogous, and made my enquiry as a private person, who had become concerned with these questions in the first place merely through my desire to find out what had happened to my personal friend, "Madeleine," a member of the "Prosper" network in France. The trail of "Madeleine" had led me inevitably into the heart of the "Prosper" network itself and the sombre mysteries surrounding its downfall, which I now believed to be due to the activities of one "Gilbert," a German agent. I would be interested to know whether I was correct in supposing that the first German contact with "Gilbert" had been made by Christmann, and would be very grateful to him if he could give me the address of Christmann, and also if he would see me himself.

After a certain delay a letter came from Germany, and it was, indeed, from the Colonel. He had, he said, been much interested in mine, but had been unable to reply earlier since I had not put my address on it. This had come about because I had sent the draft to Ernest to put into German for me and then simply signed the sheet he sent me back and re-posted it instead of copying it on to my own notepaper. The Colonel had, nevertheless, he said, gathered from the text that I was an author and had asked a literary agent to find by whom my books were published; he had now been supplied with the name and address of my publishers, care of whom he was addressing me, and hoped that his reply would reach me safely. He saw no reason why Christmann should be unwilling to see me, and in any case he, himself, would be pleased to do so if I cared to visit him at his home in Germany.

I asked him to book a room for me not too far from his own residence. He had given me no indication of where Christmann lived and this created a practical difficulty as regards the purchase of my ticket, since I was anxious to buy all the travelling involved out of British currency. The Colonel lived in the North of Germany and Ernest, whom I wanted to see again, in the South; I had to explain to the perplexed assistant in the travel agency that I wanted a ticket that would be available also to some other place I did not know. 'It sounds like a mystery tour,' he said. I finally bought a cross-country one that would take me all the way from the Colonel's home in the North to Ernest's in the South, via the Rhine, on the principle that 'quite a lot of German towns are on the Rhine,' and that anyway this route, bisecting the country like a kind of spine, would provide a possibility of getting off and taking a branch line from one of its many nodules.

This was to be my first visit to the Northern part of Germany. On August 21st I made the flight by *Lufthansa* and was more than grateful when the Colonel introduced himself at the airport and helped me through the language difficulties of the Customs; his sister was with him, and they drove me in his car to the little *pension* where he had booked me accommodation. It was she who acted, practically, as interpreter, for the Colonel's English, as he now explained to me, was of the same order as my German; he could read it, but had had little contact with English people, and could only with difficulty muster a sentence. With a twinkle in the eye, he confessed that the receipt of a letter from England asking such specific questions and bearing no address for reply had rather tickled his curiosity and stimulated him to discover the source from whence it originated.

He could give me an appointment for Tuesday afternoon, when another former officer of the *Abwehr*, Herr Huntermann, would be present to act as interpreter.

The Monday was not lost, for his sister took charge of me and showed me the town; the weather was glorious and, with the sun glittering upon the water suggested a trip by boat. I had one trouble: a briefcase. It contained a first draft of the manuscript which I intended to show Ernest and felt much too confidential to leave in an hotel bedroom. When we went back to the Colonel's flat, in his absence, for tea, his sister suggested that I could leave it there, during my stay, for safe keeping. I knew she was innocent of any thoughts concerning the implications such a move could have; but, on thinking about it, I decided that the suggestion was, in fact, good. It would, I was sure, be safe; no place, indeed, would be less likely to suffer invasion than the Colonel's flat. As I left, I passed him coming home in the evening, on the stairs, and took the occasion to explain — spacing my words out so that he could grasp each one separately — what I had done. He looked, I thought, surprised and perhaps a little troubled.

'You — may — read — it,' I said.

He did not jump at that invitation. 'It is — perhaps — better — I do not — read it. I am — not — so curious.'

'I do not — ask — do not — urge — you — to read it. I tell you only — you have my permission. It is not — secret — against you.'

'*Ich verstehen*,' he said. 'I understand.'

Next day, at five o'clock, was the big day; the meeting was at the Colonel's flat, a foursome for afternoon tea, the Colonel and his sister, Herr Huntermann, the other ex-officer from the *Abwehr*, and myself.

Whilst he had no first hand knowledge of what happened at Avenue Foch or in Kieffer's mind, the Colonel put it to me 'as a pure hypothesis' that Kieffer might have known of the "Prosper" group for some time, that he might have been content merely to keep them under observation but that some episode such as the appearance on the scene of "Anton" and Christmann had alarmed them all and forced Kieffer's hand in the sense that he was obliged to arrest them for fear they dispersed and escaped his supervision.

The Colonel had had no occasion to study the case of "Gilbert," he explained to me, but, accepting as a hypothesis and purely because I put it forward, that "Gilbert" was a German agent, he would open by asking me whether "Gilbert's" services to the *Sicherheitsdienst* were *paid*.

'I suppose so!' I said, not considering the question as of great importance.

Had I proof, he asked, that payment was made?

No. It was stated in some of the French newspapers reporting the arrest that he had been the 'highest paid German spy;' that was all I could say.

It was not sufficient, he said, though with a kindly smile. 'You have nothing official such as would be accepted in a court of law as proof of remuneration? A receipt signed by "Gilbert" for money received against services rendered to the *Sicherheitsdienst?* Or to another German department?'

I had to shake my head. Such a thing would be very difficult to obtain. It seemed to me unlikely for security reasons that he would have been required to sign a receipt.

From his smile, I perceived that he appreciated the difficulty; but I could see that something was worrying him.

'Is it important?' I asked.

'Yes,' he said briefly. 'It is important.'

He seemed to be considering with himself how he could explain something to me. It would help him to help me, he said, if I could show him the proof, not merely that "Gilbert" was a German agent but that his services to Germany had been remunerated by a German official department. If he could be satisfied of that, both formally and morally, it might be possible for him to make enquiries of some of his former colleagues as to whether they had any knowledge of the affair.

'He was not *ideological?*' he asked me at last, in this word expressing the basis of his scruples.

'I honestly do not think so.' Now that we had been talking for some time and he had got used to the sound of my voice, he told Huntermann suddenly that he could follow me (I could follow him, too, sometimes when he spoke in German.) 'Speak — very — slow — and — I — understand — all,' he said to me in English. I felt he was really pleased at this evolution; it introduced a new directness into our conversation.

'Did you have so many ideological?' I could not resist asking.

Well, he said, there were a certain number of people in the occupied countries who had genuinely believed — and who had even before the war written articles and delivered lectures maintaining — that the good of their country lay in collaboration with Germany. While such views could not commend them to the British and those of their compatriots who fought on with the British, from the German point of view these people came into a different and more sympathetic category from paid traitors. He would not wish to procure information to be used against a man who was a friend to Germany. He himself would not feel happy to act against a man in whose mental and emotional make-up a desire to see his people more closely linked with her played any part. It was a question of the man's heart. Was he a Germanophile of the heart, or simply an opportunist ready to take money from any country and owing loyalty to none? In the latter case he would not feel the same scruples and would not consider that the Germans were under a moral obligation to protect him.

He wished he could have talked with Keiffer about this. It was no secret that the *Sicherheitsdienst* and the *Abwehr* had not enjoyed the best relations; nevertheless, confronted by an enquiry from a person of Allied nationality, he would, as a German, have liked to know how Kieffer felt about this man (assuming, solely because I maintained it, the truth of the hypothesis that he was Kieffer's agent) before making up his mind what his own attitude should be.

'But you told me that you were already in relation with Kieffer's interpreter,' he said suddenly. An interpreter often knew much about the way of thinking, and way of feeling, of his chief. 'Does he not remember if Kieffer ever made reference to sums of money paid to "Gilbert"?'

I had to shake my head. 'No. I asked him once, and he said he knew nothing of any payment made to him.'

'Ask him again, will you? If he could recall even a half-phrase pronounced at some time by Kieffer, of such a character as to suggest that "Gilbert" was in receipt of payment, it would have great importance. It would help me to help you.'

'I will ask him, but I know it will be useless,' I said. 'If he remembered anything of the kind, I am sure he would have told me when I asked him first.' I could, however, assure him that such words of Kieffer as Ernest had reported to me were not of a character to suggest that "Gilbert" was moved by love for Germany or ideological considerations. Kieffer had said, 'He betrays the English and his own compatriots to us, he would betray us to them the day that it suited him better.'

'I will give you the possibility to contact Christmann,' the Colonel said. As a German, I must understand that for him the well-being of Germany must in natural loyalty take precedence over other considerations. But that having been said, he wished also the well-being of Britain and France, and men of this kind were of no use to any country. He could not give me Christmann's address, but he would give me the address of a friend of his, also an ex-officer of the *Abwehr*, in Bonn, who would be able to give me the address of Christmann. He would write a letter to his friend in Bonn, telling him to expect my arrival.

Before I left, Herr Huntermann, who had been Colonel Giskes's adjutant, gave me one piece of information, of which he authorised me to cite him as the source. He remembered names given in the radio message they had received from London: "Marcel" and "Gilbert." These were the contacts "Anton" was instructed to meet in Paris. He recollected also that word had been received by Colonel Giskes and himself from London warning them of the arrest of "Anton" even before they had received confirmation from Christmann and "Anton" that the operation had gone according to plan!

Before I left the Colonel said he thought it preferable that his name should not be mentioned excepting to his friend in Bonn.

I took the train early next morning, relieved that Bonn, at least, was on the Rhine route. At the house I was received with courtesy.

'The Colonel has explained the matter to you?' I asked the head of the family.

'No. He explained nothing. He asked me to receive you, that is all; I wait to hear what I can do for you.'

Now that I had to explain I felt the atmosphere become rather sticky. He acknowledged that he was, in fact, "Anton" who had gone with Christmann to the rendezvous at the Square Clignancourt: or more correctly, the bogus "Anton," since there existed a real Dutchman bearing this code-name sitting in prison. But more than that he would not say. He would ask me to forgive him for not wishing to discuss the details of the operation or the implications it might have had; the end, so far as his mission was concerned, was to be arrested in view of members of the "French Section." This had been staged and beautifully accomplished in the restaurant Les Capucines before Marcel, Alain and others. He had not met "Gilbert" and could not say if Christmann had done so. He would give me the address of Christmann, and it would be for him to decide whether he wished to speak of these matters.

'You will have dinner with us,' he said; and that terminated the interview. During dinner conversation was kept at a social level and I could not but admire the skill with which he had contrived to tell me nothing further while remaining a perfect host. However, I respected his reserve. 'You will tell Christmann you come from the Colonel?' he asked.

'The Colonel seemed to think it more advisable it should not go beyond yourself.'

This seemed to trouble him. 'Try to tell him,' he said. I felt that would make me disloyal to the Colonel who seemed to count on me not to do so.

'I see. It is difficult.' He got up from the table and went to his writing desk. 'I will write a letter for you to give to Christmann,' he said. He gave it to me in its envelope, with the name and address of Christmann on the outside.

So, the next day again, I departed by an early morning train for a further town, arriving in the early afternoon. Here I bought a street map, located the street upon it, and set off. I found the house, but when I looked at the names of the occupants of the different flats, I could not see the name of Christmann. Some people came out and I asked them, in halting German, which bell I should press for Christmann. They told me that all the numbers in the street had recently been put up by twelve, and advised me to go twelve houses higher up the road. I did so, but here again the name of Christmann was unknown, and I was advised, for reasons I could not understand, to go to the hairdresser's nearby. The proprietor took me to the door and pointed to a block of houses further down the road on the other side. I went to the one he had indicated but again the name of Christmann did not figure outside; I rang one of the bells but the occupant could tell me nothing. I tried the two houses on either side, walking all the way up each and trying all the bells in turn. No luck. Disconsolate and somewhat at a loss, I walked back to the hairdresser's.

This time one of his clients spoke up. He was sure it was No. 127, in the direction I had just come from but on the other side of the road. Back I went. Still no better luck, excepting in as much that the man whose bell I pressed advised me to go to the Police Station and pointed out its location to me on my map. A considerable walk to get to the Police Station, and considerable trouble in making myself understood when I got there. They got out their files, and then one of them began making extraordinary movements with one arm whilst holding the other out in front of him. He kept repeating '*Musike?*' until I realised that he was playing a violin in mime. I shook my head. '*Nein.*'

'*Welche Beruf?*' ('What profession?')

I did not want to say former officer of the *Abwehr* in case they wondered what all this was about, and stammered '*Ich weiss nicht.*' ('I don't know.')

After some consultation amongst themselves, they instructed me to go back to number 127 of the street I had just left — the very house I had just left. Rebellion in my heart, I retraced my dusty steps to that house and tried a different bell. In this flat the name of Christmann was, for the first time, known; but he had left some years ago, it was explained to me, and I should proceed to a baker's shop, in another street, and enquire there. Map in hand, I succeeded in finding the street and the baker's shop, and there again I asked for Herr Christmann. The woman wafted me with a gesture to the floor above, and in great hope I rang the bell. A woman who looked like the daily-help answered it. 'Does Herr Christmann live here?' I asked.

Yes, Herr Christmann lived here. But he was out.

When would he return?

She did not know.

'I will wait,' I said.

She did not — probably had not the right to — invite me in, and closed the door. I inspected the stairs. The wait might be long and I wanted to sit down. But the stairs were uncovered and dusty, and I was wearing my best pink and white summer frock. After some consideration I folded the coat I was carrying over my arm, so as to expose the smallest possible area, and sat on it. After about half or three-quarters of an hour, the woman looked out again and, seeing me still there, took pity on me. With the aid of gestures, she told me that she thought she knew where Herr Christmann was to be found, and beckoned me to follow her.

We walked a long way, me still clutching my precious briefcase and by this time distinctly foot-sore. At last we came to a public park with a boating lake. With a cry of triumph, my guide led me up to a bench on which sat a youth of about seventeen years old. 'Herr Christmann!'

He was a generation too young. Now what was I going to do? Perhaps he was the son of the Christmann I wanted. The envelope I carried in my bag was addressed to Richard Christmann, so I asked the youth: 'Is your father's first name Richard?'

'*Nein.*'

Deadlock.

His father was a musician, he volunteered, and was now away on tour with the orchestra to which he belonged.

I did not like to ask him whether his father had been in the *Abwehr*, so I asked him whether his father had been a soldier and where he had served during the war.

The reply was obviously inconsonant with the career of the Christmann I was seeking. I had been put into contact with the wrong family. Apologising to the youth for having disturbed him, I went away and found a seat somewhere else in the park, and sat down to rest and to think.

I got out my map of the town again and began studying it square by square to see whether there were not two streets of the same name or closely resembling names. And suddenly I found one very clearly resembling it: indeed, it was spelled just the same excepting that it had an extra syllable in the middle. Perhaps "Anton" had made a simple and easy mistake in addressing the envelope. This street I had just discovered on the map was in a suburb on the far outskirts of the town so, hobbling back to the road, for I had painful blisters by this time, I hailed the first taxi which passed and instructed the driver to take me there. This town, as I knew from its repute, was one famed for its old world charm and the beauty of its architecture; but the streets through which I had tramped ever since I arrived were neither old-world nor blessed with architectural or any other form of beauty; neither were those through which we sped in the taxi, but I enjoyed the travelling in an upholstered seat. It was a short street, and when we got to it, and cruised along it looking at the numbers, it proved not to have a number as high as that on my precious envelope. So here again I was at a dead end.

I hung on to the taxi whilst I thought. To give up without having found Christmann was unthinkable. But I could think of no further avenues to follow up in this town. It would be necessary to make contact with "Anton" again. But my heart quailed before the prospect of the long journey back to Bonn to find that not very forthcoming man again. Equally, it would be useless to try to telephone him. Not only did I not know his telephone number, but if the experiences of the last few hours had taught me that I could make myself understood to Germans in their own language when face to face, and follow their answers, I could never succeed in ringing up the directory and obtaining the number of an address in another town, far less in understanding complicated directions from "Anton" over the long-distance line from Bonn even if I could get through to him. And then I thought of Ernest. Ernest could do it for me. To Ernest's home was nearly twice the distance by rail to Bonn, in the opposite direction, but at least I would be travelling towards someone I knew well; and I had intended going on to Ernest, in the end, after I had seen Christmann.

So I told the taxi driver to take me back into the centre of the town and put me down at a Post Office. There I sent a telegram to Ernest telling him that I would be arriving ahead of schedule, by the first available train. Thence I made my way back to the station, found to my huge relief that there was an express just leaving. I arrived late at night.

There was no Ernest on the platform, and I rather thought there would have been if he had received my wire. But I took a taxi to his address as the obvious first port of call. There was no answer when I rang the bell and there were no lights in the flat above. 'Supposing they have gone away,' I thought, 'then I am really sunk.'

Eventually a young man put his head out from one of the other windows. 'They are not at home,' he said, which was obviously true. But he came down, throwing a coat over his pyjamas, and crossed the street to knock up the people in the hotel opposite, to enquire if they could give me a room. They had one free. Relieved in a way, finding myself back in an hotel where I had stayed before and the surroundings were at least familiar, I settled down to a very despondent night.

In the morning (Saturday) it was all cleared up. Ernest and his wife were home. He was on annual leave and they had been out on an all-day excursion into the country, only getting back late at night. Finding my telegram, they had been over to the hotel and enquired whether I had arrived, there, and on being told that I had, and had gone to bed, had decided not to disturb me.

And now I poured out to sympathetic ears the long recital of my woes of the day before. It was not without its comic side;

but I could see that Ernest, who curiously enough had never met or even heard of "Anton" or Christmann (or anything about the business at Square Clignancourt), was worried. He did not altogether like the sound of it. I might have been given a fictitious address, he feared. I did not think that; "Anton's" manner had been serious.

'Or it might be just a letter-box,' he suggested.

I supposed that his experience during the war prompted this line of thought.

'You don't know what you are getting into,' he said, obviously uneasy. 'It could be anything in the world.'

But somehow I did not think it was a letter-box either. "Anton" had said that Christmann was laid-up in bed, as the result of an accident, and would perforce be at home at any hour of the day for that reason. I thought the instructions given me had been genuine enough, but that there had been some mistake. Would he telephone to Bonn and speak to "Anton" for me. He was not really very eager; he did not want to 'get mixed up' in something he did not understand and wished that I, too, would give the whole thing up. But in the end, kindly, he came with me to the Post Office, rang up the directory, obtained the number in Bonn and put through a personal trunk call. Standing with him in the box, I could understand something of the conversation which ensued.

'He says the address he gave you was correct,' he told me, 'but he says you should not ask for Christmann, you should ask for the lady he is staying with. He thought he had explained that.'

So that was the solution. I could feel that Ernest was still only half assured that all was well, but I told him I would write a letter to Christmann, care of the lady as instructed, and send it by Express post (delivered in Germany on a Sunday) asking him to reply by telegram if he was able to see me on Monday.

As we walked back from the Post Office, Ernest asked me suddenly, 'Did you *see* the letter which you are carrying before it was put into the envelope?'

It was curious that he should ask me that. I had had a dream about that envelope, which suggested a suppressed disquiet as to its contents, though I had not worried consciously.

'No.'

'And the envelope is sealed?'

'Yes. Do you think the letter advises him not to tell too much?'

He smiled a little. 'It could do. It would be quite easy to steam it open so that it would hardly be noticed, but I suppose we have to behave decently. Let us hope it is all right.'

After lunch I asked him once more, since the Colonel had asked me to, whether he had ever heard if "Gilbert" was in receipt of remuneration.

No, he said. He had never heard of a reason suggested for "Gilbert's" rendering the services he did to the Germans. He rendered them, that was all. Quite honestly, he had never heard money spoken of in connection with "Gilbert"; perhaps it was only in order to be able to receive and dispatch his aircraft in peace. He recollected no phrase spoken by either Kieffer or any of his colleagues which could have reference to payments made. All he could say on this head was negative; he had never heard anybody at the Avenue Foch credit "Gilbert" with genuine friendship or loyalty toward the Germans, or with ideological promptings. He was regarded as an adventurer, and as self-interested. Kieffer never trusted him.

He read through the manuscript (which bore little resemblance to the present book except in its basic substance) and made a few corrections regarding *Sicherheitsdienst* ranks, titles and the like. 'You will have difficulty in getting it published,' was his only comment.

We spoke of Madame Aigrain and he readily confirmed that he had been her interrogator. She had been a most uncooperative prisoner. He remembered very clearly the Andrès' report. The whole message had been upon a single sheet of paper. It was indeed a report concerning the effects of the bombing of Boulogne-sur-Seine and Courbevoie. Nothing else. It was signed at the foot, Sander, which he took to be an anagram for Andrès. But he had asked both Andrès and Madame Aigrain to copy out something in their own hands, to be quite sure that it was he and not she who had written it. Kieffer had given him the photostat after "Madeleine's" arrest, with instructions to show it to "Madeline". Madame Aigrain and Andrès had been captured just prior to "Madeleine" but, if he remembered rightly, the photostat had been given him in the first place to show to "Madeline" and afterwards he had on his own initiative shown it to Madame Aigrain and to Andrès separately.

I think nobody was more surprised than Ernest when, on Sunday afternoon, a telegram came for me at my hotel, from Christmann, giving me an appointment at the original address for five o'clock on Monday afternoon. 'So it was genuine after all,' he said.

On the morning of Monday, August 29th, Ernest saw me to the station, hoped gallantly that he was being an unnecessarily gloomy prophet, and wished me luck both in the forthcoming interview with Christmann and the eventual publication of the manuscript.

CHAPTER NINE: CHRISTMANN

And so, shortly after five o'clock, I found myself back at the house where my search of the previous Friday had begun. I knew which bell to press this time, and a young girl let me in and introduced me to a room in which a blond and still youngish man was lying in bed. He apologised in perfect French for having to receive me in this condition, explaining that he had been knocked down by a car whilst crossing the road and suffered a severe injury to his spine, which had necessitated an operation, and that in the circumstances he was obliged to stay at his fiancée's home in order that she might tend him. He performed the introductions. 'Did you think there was some mystery about this address?' he asked.

'Yes,' I confessed. 'I wondered if it was a letter-box!'

He laughed; no, the explanation was, as I saw, purely personal. 'Now I will tell you one thing,' he said. 'When you are in Germany and you want to find somebody, if you know the town you have only to go to the Police Station. That is what you should have done.'

I told him I *had* done; he could make nothing of it. His fiancée had, by this time, melted tactfully away, and we got down to business. In my letter I had said only that I would like him to tell me of his relations in 1943, with "Gilbert", without specifying which "Gilbert" I meant. Now he asked me, 'When you say "Gilbert", whom do you mean?'

'Both of them,' I said, taking the bull by the horns.

He looked at me very narrowly, obviously trying to size me up, and asked me what I was talking about and where I had got his name.

After what Ernest had said, I was not too eager to present the letter of introduction I carried from "Anton" though I had mentioned in mine that I had one. I would, I decided, not proffer it unless he asked for it. I told him that I was not acting for any official service or organisation, had never belonged to the "French Section" or any department of S.O.E., but had been, in private life, the friend of "Madeleine", a young girl who had served with the "Prosper" network; that after the war I had been to France in the endeavour to find out what had happened to her, and that my researches had led me into an independent enquiry into the betrayal and downfall of the whole "Prosper" network. I had discovered his name from a copy, which had been shown me unofficially by a French Abbé living in the country, of a deposition which he had made to the French authorities.

'Which one?' he asked. 'They are not all reliable.'

I told him it was made before a Captain Trossin.

That one was reasonably all right, he thought, as far as he remembered. 'What did I say in it?'

I told him.

'Yes, that is correct enough,' he said.

'But I feel that it is not the whole story,' I said. 'You write that you were instructed by your Chief to make contact with "Gilbert" who would arrange the air-transport of "Anton" from Paris to London. Instead, you were put into contact, by mistake, with "Gilbert-Archambault", who had nothing to do with air transport. Surely you could not have left it there? You would not have wanted to go back to your Chief and report that you had not found the right man? You would have tried to find him. I would like to know whether you did find him, and what happened.'

He scrutinised me, his face alive with curiosity and suspicion. 'Why do you want to know about these things? Tell me frankly.'

I put it to him that the meeting he had had with "Gilbert-Archambault" alias Gilbert Norman, under a misunderstanding, could reflect adversely upon Norman, unless the circumstances were fully understood.

'If it is to clear Norman, then I am willing!' he said relieved. 'Norman was ignorant that I was a German.'

'And the other Gilbert?' I asked.

His relief faded as quickly. 'Is this to clear Norman or to accuse the other?'

'The two things go together,' I said. 'They are two parts of one story, which interlock.'

He did not like this. He would be a willing witness for the clearance of an innocent man, he said, but he would not wish to be a party to an accusation. 'Tell me, I beg you, what you are driving at, Mademoiselle. Is it to clear Norman or to accuse the other? I adore frankness!'

Lamely, I began to talk to him about Gilbert Norman's father.

'What was Gilbert Norman to you?' he asked.

'I never knew him. I know only his father, whom I met less than a year ago.' Mr. Norman, I explained, was an elderly man, to whom the death of his son had been a heavy grief, the bitterness of that grief had been aggravated by rumours which circulated in some quarters impinging upon the honour of his dead boy; his distress had affected me and I was trying to clear the honour of the dead for the father's sake.

Suddenly he lost patience. 'This is a cover-story,' he said. 'What about telling me the truth?'

Confused, but unable to refrain from laughing, I declared, 'It is quite true, so far as it goes! I really do know Mr. Norman and I really am concerned for him.'

'But you have not come half way across Germany and taken all these pains on account of the aged father of a man you never knew. Come, Mademoiselle, tell me your real motive!'

This was an appeal for a deep answer. 'I hardly know you,' I fenced.

'It is you who want something from me, Mademoiselle. If you want me to disclose something you must first disclose your own position.'

I knew nothing of him except that he had been a double-agent and to discuss some things with a German was in any case difficult. I stammered as much.

He lay back on his pillows a trifle huffily. 'It is for you to decide,' he said, 'whether you can trust me.'

I took the plunge and spoke sincerely and simply of the things that weighed on my mind and heart. Suddenly he stopped me.

'I trust you,' he said. And he gave me his hand to shake. 'I have confidence in you. Sometimes one has to make up one's mind very quickly. But now what am I going to tell you? With the best will in the world, it is not so easy.'

'When you made those depositions you were a prisoner,' I said, 'and being a prisoner, you may have felt under a certain compulsion to write something, even if you did not wish to lay the matter bare. Now you are not a prisoner and you are under no compulsion to tell me anything at all. If you do not wish to, I will simply go away. All I ask you is that if you do tell me something, it will be true. And that you will not choose your words so as to mislead me.'

He seemed almost distressed. But his distress was, in itself, an earnest that my appeal had struck home into his being. Nothing glib rose to his lips. I must understand, he said, that the *métier* of double-agent was complicated. And when one had been engaged at the same time in a contraband traffic in gold and gems, that further increased the complexity of one's life. It was sometimes difficult to pick out and relate the exact truth concerning even a single episode without opening the door to questions concerning other matters one would not wish to disclose. If I would give him a little time in which to reflect, he would think how much there was that he could tell me, that would be true and not misleading, without uncovering more than he wanted.

'I understand,' I said, and settled myself in quietness for a long wait. That he had spoken already so honestly was, in itself, an assurance that what would come would also be honest.

'I can do it!' he exclaimed suddenly, after the lapse of a shorter time than I had expected to have to wait. 'It can be isolated. It is quite detachable.'

He had, of course, served under Colonel Giskes in Holland and was 'in the know' concerning the great *Nordpol* operation. For about a year, London had never asked for the return of any of the agents it parachuted out, who were, of course, imprisoned on arrival; when London suddenly issued an order for "Anton" to return, a new situation was created. The real "Anton" could not, of course, be released from prison, yet prevarication might cause suspicion. Colonel Giskes therefore decided that one of his own men should play the role of "Anton", go to Paris as instructed by London, with Christmann as guide, and meet the man London required; after which the arrest of Colonel Giskes's "Anton" must be staged with the cooperation of German services in Paris in view of members of the "French Section", who must be allowed to escape his fate by a hair's breadth, and who could be expected to inform their chiefs in London (as indeed they did) of what had happened. The failure of "Anton" to reappear in London would thus be explained without suspicion being brought to bear upon the network in Holland.

London had informed *Nordpol* that the contact in Paris, who would arrange for the departure by air of "Anton" was one "Gilbert"; the message received from London instructed them to contact "Gilbert" at a house in the Square Clignancourt on a certain day at a certain time and to speak a certain password when in the presence of "Gilbert." It was in the morning and the day was a Thursday; it was towards the end of May, though he would not be able to give the date without reference to a calendar for 1943. Say, offhand, the last Thursday in May.

He and the bogus "Anton" had proceeded together to the Square Clignancourt, but "Anton" alone had entered the house, whilst he had remained outside, in the close vicinity. After a while, "Anton" had come out again, accompanied by three other men, who were in fact, "Archambault", Alain and Marcel [Charbonnier]. They had come up to him, and "Archambault" had said, 'I'm Gilbert but I'm not the Gilbert you want. There has been some mistake.' He had explained that Gilbert was his own Christian name, but not his code-name with the "French Section." His colleagues generally called him Gilbert, informally, and that was doubtless how the confusion had arisen. For there undoubtedly had been a confusion.[44] He had nothing whatever to do with air transport

---

[44] There may have been more confusion than he (or I at the time of our conversation) knew. I learned later that "Marcel" was the official code-name of Major Agazarian, whose mission with Major Boddington had not been his first. Agazarian alias "Marcel" had been in France and in contact with "Gilbert", the Air Movements Officer,

and knew nothing of the arrangements concerning it. There was, however, another man who had the official code-name of "Gilbert", and who was, in fact, charged with all responsibilities concerning the arrival and departure of "French Section" agents by air. It was certainly this man whom he and "Anton" had been supposed to meet and he would try to get hold of him during the course of the day.

'"Archambault" was certainly ignorant that "Anton" and I were Germans. That I can swear,' Christmann said, very earnestly. 'He was a clean man.'

A rendezvous between Christmann and "Archambault" had been convened for the afternoon in a café. "Archambault" had turned up at the time agreed, accompanied by a dark haired young girl whom he introduced as "Denise." He had, he said, made contact with "Gilbert," who had said he was sorry he had not come to the Square Clignancourt that morning but he had been too busy; he had, for the same reason, been unable to accompany "Archambault" to the present meeting point and regretted that he would be unable to offer "Anton" and himself a rendezvous for two or three days; after which he would communicate.

"Archambault" delivered this as being a straightforward statement from "Gilbert", but to Christmann, as he listened, it did not sound so straightforward. Was "Gilbert", he wondered, being on the level with "Archambault"? The excuse of his

---

at the time of the Clignancourt mix-up, and used at this time to transmit for him. Indeed, he might have been considered at this period as virtually "Gilbert's" radio operator. Perhaps he rather than Marcel Charbonnier (who had no contact with "Gilbert", the Air Movements Officer) was the intended "Marcel" whose name was coupled with that of "Gilbert" in the message from London remembered by Huntermann. We have now a *Comedy of Errors* type of situation: two "Marcels" attached to two "Gilberts."

being 'too busy' seemed to him unnatural. To a genuine "French Section" agent, an order from London would be a priority. Especially an order of this kind, to be at a certain place at a certain precise time to meet a man who had come from Holland and who could only make his identity known by the utterance of a certain sentence communicated in advance by London to both parties independently. A genuine agent could never treat such an order in so cavalier a manner; if he had, through some quite unforeseen and unavoidable mishap, been prevented from keeping the original rendezvous, he would certainly have hastened to repair the damage by availing himself instantly of the opportunity afforded him by "Archambault's" intervention, for a second rendezvous. There was something wrong with "Gilbert."

'It occurred to me that he might be a German agent,' Christmann said to me.

'But how could you leap to such a conclusion?' I asked. 'You had nothing to go on! Nothing to suggest *that*.'

'I don't know how to put it into words,' he said. 'I have a nose, and I smelled something!'

In this kind of work, he had learned to trust his instinctive sense of a situation. Proof was often impossible and one had to frame one's actions with regard to what one's inner sense told one to be the case. While "Archambault" was talking, he had had, therefore, to work out a complicated series of possibilities in his own mind and decide what he should do. If "Gilbert" were, unknown to "Archambault" and "Denise" and the others, a German agent, like himself, then there was the question as to whether or not they should disclose themselves to one another, privately, in their true character. But "Gilbert" could hardly be an *Abwehr* agent, or he and the bogus "Anton" would have been told about him before they set out; they would have been told that the "French Section" 'contact' was really one of themselves. Since they had not been told, the probability was that he was an agent of the *Sicherheitsdienst*, therefore of Sturmbannführer Kieffer. Now the question was, did he want to act in open concert with an agent of the *Sicherheitsdienst*? Did he want to disclose his own identity as an *Abwehr* agent to an agent of the *Sicherheitsdienst*? And, if they neither of them disclosed themselves, would it not be somewhat farcical for two German agents, belonging to different services, to meet and hold conversation in solemn maintenance of their respective guises as Allied agents?

All this had to be thought out almost in a flash, for "Archambault" must not notice anything preoccupied or suspicious in his own manner. He decided that he did not want to become mixed up with an agent of the *Sicherheitsdienst* and said to "Archambault", as naturally as he could, that he and "Anton" had talked it over and come to the conclusion that it was not necessary for them to meet "Gilbert" at all, as they had a possibility of making other arrangements.

That was that. "Archambault" did not seem to suspect anything peculiar in his own crying-off.

Christmann had not exploited his contact with "Archambault" and "Denise" because it was not to the interest of Operation *Nordpol* that they should be arrested; he had not been sent to France to bring about the arrest of a group of "French Section" agents, but solely in the interest of the security of the *Nordpol* operation and that would not be served by a series of arrests following the appearance on the scene of "Anton" and himself.

Some two or three, or three or four, days later, he had, however, occasion to call in at the Avenue Foch to see Kieffer.

Wishing to verify his hunch, he said suddenly, 'So, you have an agent called "Gilbert!"'

Kieffer had fallen to his bluff, and said that it was most important this should not become known. Sensing from Kieffer's gravity that a matter of considerable weight hung upon this agent's security, he hastened to assure him of his utmost discretion. Kieffer, however, was obviously concerned that even he should have rifled the secret, and asked him in what manner he had come to divine "Gilbert's" true role. He endeavoured to allay Kieffer's disquiet by assuring him that he had had really nothing to go on; but he had the impression that Kieffer felt almost as if a breach in security had occurred, and that "Gilbert's" position was not so safe as before.

So I had been wrong in thinking that Christmann had been "Gilbert's" first German contact. But the truth was even more interesting. 'So you never, in fact, met "Gilbert"?' I asked.

'No. Not really...' (There was a slight hesitation here. I wondered what it covered, but did not press.) He had, he said, been interrogated concerning him by the French almost immediately after his arrest (he was arrested only on the anniversary of V.E. day). He had prevaricated and refused to own to any knowledge of "Gilbert." Later, in November, 1947, he had been confronted with "Gilbert" at the D.S.T. and asked again, in his presence, whether he had any knowledge of him, or concerning him. Again he had denied it.

'But why? Why did you not tell them what you knew?' I burst out, beside myself.

'It was not my role!' he exclaimed, wide-eyed. 'I am a German! It was not my part to assist the French in their enquiries!' He had realised that the confusion of the two "Gilberts" in respect of the meeting at the Square Clignancourt had confused the French authorities also; they did not understand the precise nature of what had happened and their lack of certainty had left a doubt hanging over two men. He had phrased his answers so as to leave that doubt.

'But that was not fair to the memory of Gilbert Norman,' I protested.

He had thought it was more important to save a live man than the honour of a dead one. If Norman had been alive, it would have been different. He begged me to believe that he would never have borne witness against a live man of a nature to cause him to be charged with a crime of which he knew him to be innocent. 'But *I knew that he was dead and it could not hurt him.*'

I knew, too, that while this argument might be felt as offensive by many, he was sincere in it. I said, very gently, that it had hurt the father.

He had not thought of the possibility of its getting back to the family, to affect them. 'I had not thought so far.' This was said very simply, and I knew that it was true. 'I am very sorry,' he said. 'Will you explain this to Norman's father, and ask him to forgive me if he can?'

'I will do so,' I said. But I felt that a difficult charge was devolving upon me. 'I am afraid he will take it bitterly, but I will put it as nicely as I can.'

'Thank you, he said. 'I would not have caused pain willingly. It was only because it was the only way I could see to save "Gilbert". Not simply because "Gilbert" was a German agent, he said, but because he was a human being who was still alive. He had known a lot of death. It was oppressive. And, in the fetid atmosphere of accusations and counter-accusations which followed the war, to save at least someone had seemed 'the better part.'

'He gave me a little present afterwards,' he said. At least, a little present had been delivered to him in his cell some time afterwards, with a scrap of paper inside on which was written one word only: Merci. He could not think who else should want to say 'Thank you' to him, and he thought it must be from "Gilbert."

I could see that he felt some sentiment about this; it was indeed the only sympathetic thing I had ever heard about "Gilbert", for it suggested a capacity for gratitude. I could feel that Christmann was troubled by the thought that now he had let him down.

He had grown thirsty, and called for his fiancée to fetch us some beer. She did so, joined us for a glass and disappeared again. He pulled up the side of his mattress and produced a packet of cigarettes from underneath it and an ash-tray full of stubs. 'I am forbidden by the doctor to smoke,' he explained, as he offered me a cigarette. 'That's why I have to hide them from Eva.'

'But you have a letter for me!' he exclaimed suddenly.

Nemesis. I took the envelope from my bag and handed it to him, and waited in anxious suspense whilst he broke it open and took the letter out and began to read. He chuckled. 'He has a nice way of expressing his sympathy, he says this will teach me to give up jay-walking in the future!' He went on reading. Then suddenly he started, and looked at me with wide eyes. 'Oh! So you have seen the Colonel!'

So *that* was what "Anton" had done. I felt mean now, for Christmann had given me much of his confidence and my silence had put me in a false position.

'The Colonel did not wish too wide publicity to be given to our interview; that was why I was not sure whether I should mention his name even to you,' I said, trying to put it tactfully.

He gave me the most malicious twinkle, as though to say that he knew perfectly well that he had been discriminated against. But to my immense relief, he did not seem to hold it against me. I began to laugh, and he laughed too.

Coming back to what I knew was troubling him, he begged me not to think the worst of "Gilbert." It was possible that he had worked for the Allies after all, and that he might have used his relations with the *Sicherheitsdienst* to the ultimate profit of Britain. If he informed London concerning all that he learned from his contacts with the German services, then he could be a very powerful agent for London. 'He could have been one of your most brilliant double-agents!'

I hated to seem uncharitable, but I had to say that I did not think that this, in fact, was how it was. All my information led me to suppose that he had worked to the German profit.

Even if that were so, he might, Christmann pleaded, have had some *idea* in his mind of ultimately turning things to the profit of his rightful chiefs in Britain. Or he might have had some such idea when he started, even if he had not been able to carry it through. Even if, whilst playing the part of a double-agent, he had got carried into a further degree of collaboration with the Germans than he had intended at the start, he might always have thought of himself, in his heart, as a British agent. Would I not admit this more charitable interpretation, or, since we could not know the truth, at least give it a place in my considerations, along with others?

'I could give it place in my book as a quote from you,' I said at last. 'I would be willing to do that, if it would make you happier. I know that you are trying to make a case for him because you feel in duty bound, and because you hate to do him an injury. But if I put it in my book, I shall have to make it plain that it comes from you and not from me.'

He still went on pleading. We did not know how the whole thing had begun. We did not know that "Gilbert" had walked into a German office one day, as a free man, and said he wished to sell his own country and England for money. It did not usually happen like that. There were a hundred and one paths by which a man might come to end up in the service of an enemy power without having chosen it as an act of free will at the beginning. We did not know that he had accepted money. He might have been under some form of compulsion, blackmail, threats to his family, or even beating. Supposing that he had fallen into the hands of one of the more vile gangs which operated under the control of certain German services and been unmercifully beaten, would I still cast stones at a man who had yielded in a moment of weakness under pressure of physical pain, and who afterwards had to carry on because, having once 'faulted' he dared not confess to his chiefs in London?

All this was heart-rending and making me feel as though I were coldly unmerciful. But I had to maintain my loyalties as he maintained his. 'Look here,' I said, 'I am nearer in natural sympathy to those whom he betrayed to their deaths, and it is unfair to try to wring my heart for "Gilbert." You mustn't try to make me feel a brute because I can't feel about him as you do. I can promise you that I will not write vindictively concerning him. I shall put only the facts which we know, without seeking to show his motives as being either the lowest, or the better or more pitiable which you suggest to me, and without seeking in any way to interpret his heart or the state of his conscience.'

'I only want to say,' he said, 'that *I* do not want to *judge* "Gilbert." I feel that he may be something the same kind of man as myself.'

I realised this was a genuine sentiment and expressed perhaps the quick of his feeling in the matter.

'I think you are doing yourself an injustice,' I said gently. 'There is a great difference. You were not a traitor to your own country. You were acting for it.'

He nodded. He had never acted, except in semblance, for the Allies. He would never, in any circumstances, betray Germany. But the life of a double-agent was full of shifts and manoeuvres which ran across normal morality at many points and bedevilled human relations with those whom, in other circumstances, one could have wished to have as friends. "Gilbert" had led a life, in many particulars, similar to his own, and he could only feel a fellow-feeling for him, as in a way one of his own kind. He did not want to throw stones. 'It would not become me to sit in judgment on "Gilbert." Can you understand my feelings?'

'Yes,' I said. 'I can understand.'

'I have not talked like this for years,' he said. 'Not since the war have I talked freely about these things.'

We talked after that for a long time, and about many things. He told me of other episodes in the war with which he had been concerned, but which he could not give me present leave to print. Should he ever decide that the time had come to publish them, he would ask me if I would undertake the writing. That way the bitterness would be avoided, that might be provoked by a one-sided account. He did not want to add to the legacy of bitterness between peoples that the war had left in its train; he had seen enough.

We had got so deep into human questions that it was only with an effort I later brought my mind back to the 'technical points' of the story I had come about, and which I must get clear. Why, I remembered at last to ask him, had he had to accompany the bogus "Anton" in the function of 'guide'?

He explained to me, then, an off-shoot or by-product of Operation *Nordpol*. There existed certain escape routes by which Allied nationals, most often Dutch citizens, used to pass from Holland through Belgium into France, and thence through either Spain or Switzerland to England. As his chief, Lt.-Col. Giskes, came to know of them, so they came under *Abwehr* control. Certain of these escape routes were run in conjunction with one of the groups of "Dutch Section" agents parachuted from London into Holland, and therefore met on the field by Colonel Giskes' men and transferred to prison. Lest their fate be suspected in London, their work had to be carried on in their name, by German agents, and the Allied citizens using the related escape-routes had to be allowed *really* to escape. The regularity with which they turned up in England, after a safe journey, which they could not know had been made under the wing of *Abwehr* protection, seemed to London an assurance that the group in Holland was functioning most efficiently, and was thus a valuable protection to the security of the German Operation *Nordpol*. The escape of the Allied citizens concerned did not seriously worry Germany and was a small price to pay for the security of *Nordpol*. He, Christmann, had been introduced to the organisers of the escape-routes as a 'Belgian patriot' with the name of "Arnaud." His French was perfect, and the guise of Belgian dispelled any doubts which might be created by his fair colouring and rather non-Latin appearance. London was kept regularly informed of the achievements of "Arnaud" in shepherding the escapees through from Holland across Belgium into France, and as the escapes he organised were always (naturally) successful, his credit grew and London came to place the greatest confidence in him. A medal was even parachuted out to him in appreciation of his services. London had thus been delighted to hear that their valuable man "Anton" was to be conducted all the way to Paris by "Arnaud" (Christmann).

Christmann had answered my question and explained the nature of his role; but now I was perplexed and intrigued by the reference to a medal.

'The British parachuted a medal out to you? What medal?'

He hesitated, then said almost shyly, 'The Military Cross.' He spoke the words in English, the first words he had spoken in my own language; it sounded strange coming from his lips.

He was naively curious to know the value of it as a British decoration, and what kind of services it was normally awarded for; I told him, as truly as I knew, 'It is quite high.' But I had never heard of a medal being parachuted before — and certainly not to an enemy!

He explained. In London, they did not, of course, realise that he was a German. They thought he was a Belgian patriot. As he could not desert his post in the field to come to England to receive it, they had parachuted it to him. After the war, when they realised their mistake, they had been concerned about it. A British officer had come to see him and ask for it back. It was, of course, invalid, the British officer explained; as a German he could not possibly wear a British decoration which had been awarded to him under a misunderstanding.

He was reluctant to give it up, for he had become in a way attached to it; he said he would promise not to wear it, but he would like to keep it as a souvenir.

This had not satisfied the British officer. The award would be formally cancelled in London, he said, and pointed out that it could, indeed, never have had any validity since Christmann was of enemy nationality; if he insisted on retaining it, he would be holding nothing but a little piece of metal from which all significance had been withdrawn.

In the end, he had given it back, so as not to create ill-feeling. The British officer had appeared very relieved, and had even accepted in good part the quip with which he returned it.

His bi-lingual ability in French had, in point of fact, proved a mixed blessing; it had enabled him, after the war, to hide himself in France for a year, but when he was at last discovered and arrested, his absence of German accent, combined with the really beautiful set of false papers with which he had managed to provide himself, and which made him out a Frenchman, convinced the French authorities that he was in truth French: knowing his service with the *Abwehr* they charged him with treason. Now he had considerable ado to convince them that all his false papers *were* false. He had, indeed, spent some time in the part of the prison reserved for those condemned to die before he was able, by referring them to his pre-war record of service with the French Foreign Legion in which he had registered as a German, to convince them that he was in fact German, and that what they were charging him with was 'intelligence' with his own country; when of course the charge was annulled, and it only remained to establish that, as a German soldier, he had not been connected with any war crime. It had still taken a year or two to clear his case up, but in the end they had discharged him, with a single ticket back to the Fatherland, and a guard to see him across the frontier.

A reference he had made, earlier in the evening, to gold, had intrigued me, but I had hesitated to ask him to enlarge on this. Before leaving, however, I did so. 'You mentioned, earlier, that you had at one time been concerned in a contraband traffic in gold and gems. I don't want to ask an improper question, and you need not answer it. But "Gilbert" was, at one moment, caught smuggling gold, and I would be extremely interested to know whether you were at any time acting with "Gilbert" during the war in connection with the smuggling of gold.'

'No, he said, 'I can answer that honestly. I have never acted in conjunction with "Gilbert", either in connection with the smuggling of gold or anything else. I never acted in concert with him.

I obtained his permission to print all that he had told me concerning "Gilbert" and the confusion of the two "Gilberts", and promised to type out the story as I had understood it from him and send it to him to vet.

'And I will sign it,' he said. 'That way, it will be better for you and for me.'

I left him with a warm feeling of gratitude for the confidence he had given me, and made my way back to the railway station. There I was able to catch a midnight express to the North.

My mind was too active for sleep. What Christmann had told me had, of course, invalidated the story told by "Gilbert" at his trial. "Gilbert" had told the court that the Germans had first approached him on June 2nd. I had always been curious as to why he chose that particular date; but, whatever the reason, his contact with the Germans obviously antedated June 2nd, if Christmann was right in his divination as to the reason for his failure to turn up on the last Thursday in May. And Christmann had been able to check with Kieffer, only a few days later, that he was right; it was a pity he did not know the precise date of his conversation with Kieffer, when Kieffer admitted "Gilbert" was his agent. At any rate, and without a calendar, the last Thursday in May plus a few days would bring the date precious near to June 2nd — and that was strikingly interesting. Had "Gilbert" dated his contact with the Germans from the day of Christmann's conversation with Kieffer? Or, perhaps, from the day when he was warned by his German chiefs that his relationship with them had become known to an agent outside their own service? For he might very well have been told to watch his step.

But the impact of the human situations which had arisen from my meeting with Christmann bore upon me more heavily than the technical points concerning the "Gilbert" story. What was I going to say to Mr. Norman when I wrote to him, as I must when I returned to England? What was I going to say to the Colonel, when I met him tomorrow, as I hoped, for I had promised to call on him and say goodbye on my return journey? He had not thought it necessary I should divulge his name to Christmann. If he had asked me for an absolute promise of secrecy I should have had the strength to refuse; for I had long made it my rule to give promises of secrecy to no one: experience had taught me that a promise not to tell something could place one in an awkward position if, perhaps, circumstances should arise in which an explanation seemed advisable. In the years that I had been engaged on this research, I had never once demanded secrecy of those in whom I placed my confidence and I had never acceded to such a demand from another, however much trusted. Trust, as I saw it, must in these matters, include confidence in the discretion of the person trusted. (If confidence could not be vested in the discretion of the hearer, then the confidential matter were better not communicated).

Secrecy, in the form of promises extracted, belonged to the dark side of things; it bound the giver to him to whom he gave it and, by making it impossible for him to take outside counsel, isolated him. Safety lay in keeping all the channels of communication open; and this, I felt, became in my case all the more true in proportion to the complexity of the matters in which I became involved and the need for voluntary discretion. In a research touching so often upon things which were involved and unclean, the one golden thread to which I clung for protection was the keeping of my relations with each individual honest. That way, I felt, the darkness could not seize me.

But the Colonel had limited himself to the expression of an opinion (that his name need go no further) and that had led me into this trap; he had assumed that I would abide by his obvious wish, and I, assuming him to have good reason, had intended to; in that spirit I had told "Anton" that the Colonel did not wish his name to go further. "Anton" had solved the problem, as regards his relations with Christmann, by writing the Colonel's name in the letter he gave me in a sealed envelope. In a way, he had helped me, in as much as he had allowed my relations with Christmann to gain a franker basis without *my* having to let the cat out of the bag. But what was I to tell the Colonel? I had avowed his name when Christmann read the letter and taxed me; I should be false to the Colonel if I kept silent about this, and if I told what had happened I should be 'splitting' on "Anton" and perhaps make trouble between them. But that was the way it would have to be, I decided in the end: I would tell the Colonel if he asked, and write to "Anton" to explain that it was not in malice that I had given him away!

These last years had seemed to me often like an exercise in loyalties. I received confidences from all sides, and sometimes from people who would not have given them to each other, and often going beyond what they wished me to print. I had always to think whether what I repeated could damage the teller in another quarter, or whether what seemed to me to be publishable could damage him in his own country, in other countries or with individuals. Curiously enough, the difficulties had not been so much as between French and German, as I had feared at the outset when I found myself received first in one country and then in the other. The actual combatants in the 'secret' war had less bitterness than bystanders would imagine; certainly less bitterness than the bystanders. There was between them a certain respect for the point of view of their opposite numbers, not always untouched by sympathy. My most delicate problems had concerned those on the same side of the fence: Norman and the Abbé had represented my sorest problem in France; and now, as the train rumbled northwards through the night, I had on my hands not only a passion-provoking matter which I must break to Norman in such a manner that he would forgive Christmann, but an awkward three-cornered problem involving the relations between three officers of the *Abwehr!* It was not without its comical side. It was by now daylight, and with that thought to lighten my heart, I went to look for breakfast in the dining-car.

I called on the Colonel in the afternoon, after my arrival, but he was out; so I sat on his doorstep and wrote him a short note to say I was back, and pushed it through the box. He was round at my hotel, with his car, at noon next day, to take me out to lunch. I told him what had happened with the letter and, to my great relief, he took it in a humouristic spirit. He and Christmann had not at all times enjoyed the very best relations, and he had not thought his name would help me in that quarter. 'But he received you in a friendly manner? Then that is all that matters.' And he told me to forget about it.

We lunched at an open air restaurant at a table on a lawn giving down to the lake and talked until nearly four in the afternoon, when he had to keep an appointment. Whilst he always maintained a proper reserve, I felt that he, too, had come to trust me.

Shortly after six, he called for me again and drove me in his car to the airport.

CHAPTER TEN: TO BRING MATTERS TO A HEAD

My first duty on arriving back to London was to cope with the correspondence arising out of my trip to Germany; an assurance to Ernest that I had found Christmann all right (it was curious that Christmann had never heard of Ernest any more than Ernest had heard of Christmann), a thank-you letter to the Colonel, another to "Anton" explaining that I had given his stratagem away, but that the Colonel had not appeared to take it amiss, and finally a letter to Christmann himself enclosing a typed resumé of what I had understood him to tell me at our interview.

Christmann returned the top copy of my resumé (I had told him to keep the carbon), signed at the foot of every sheet, as formally as though it were an official deposition. I was very relieved, as I had been anxious lest he have second thoughts when he saw it on paper. There were only one or two very minor corrections. The first was to his rank; I had described him as Major, following the D.S.T. deposition, and he had struck it through and put *Sonderführer*. I have never discovered a proper translation for this title, but to the best of my understanding it denotes a noncommissioned officer engaged upon duties of so specialised a nature as to render him otherwise unclassifiable. (I knew already that German N.C.O.'s could in some circumstances come to play a role of an importance out of all proportion with that one would expect of their rank).

The second correction, though small, was interesting. Following his verbal statement, I had put his conversation with

Kieffer as from two to four days after the meeting at the Square Clignancourt. He struck this through and wrote in the margin that he thought it would be truer to say a week.

The letter, dated 13th September, 1955, which he sent with the enclosures was in itself most interesting.

> 'When I was first interrogated at the D.S.T. at the end of May 1946, concerning "Gilbert," I was not confronted with him but a dozen photographs were set in front of me to see if I could pick "Gilbert" out. I was at the time half blind following a prolonged interrogation under "sunlights," and it was only with difficulty that I recognised one of the photos as being that of a man whom I had seen twice or three times on the premises (*dans les locaux*) of the S.D., Avenue Foch. It was the *Commissaire of the D.S.T.* who told me then that this was the photograph of "Gilbert." After the interrogation I was unable to read the report of what I had said and signed my so-called statement blind. After the interrogation the *Commissaire* told me that a "highly placed person of the British secret service" (he did not tell me his name) had intervened in favour of "Gilbert" but that they "would get him all the same."
>
> On Wednesday October 29th, 1947, at 10.30 I was summoned before the *Juge d'Instruction*, Captain Trossin, who interrogated me concerning "Gilbert" in the presence of Major Schafer, formerly of the *Abwehr*. It was only on 4th November 1947 that I was confronted with "Gilbert," in the office of the *Juge d'Instruction*, Trossin. When thus confronted I recognised in "Gilbert"
>
> (a) a man whom I had seen several times at liberty on the premises of the Avenue Foch

(b) the person whom I had recognised in May 1946 in one of the photographs set before me at the D.S.T.

I said nothing about that to Captain Trossin and pretended that I was now setting eyes on "Gilbert" for the first time.

I have already explained to you why I then charged poor Gilbert Norman, because I knew him to be dead.'

Ernest had told me he never saw "Gilbert" at the Avenue Foch and imagined that he always met Goetz outside. I was therefore surprised that Christmann should have seen him there. However, Ernest's knowledge was confined to No. 84; and seeing that "Gilbert" had in the first place been attached to Boemelburg in Number 82, and that he would not have been strictly speaking Kieffer's agent at the time in question, it seemed possible that Christmann might have been referring to the neighbouring house.

There was a postscript to Christmann's letter:

I ask you most urgently to explain everything to Gilbert Norman's father and ask him to forgive me if he can for lending my hand to soiling the name of his son. I thought to do right in charging a dead man to save a living one. Perhaps even he can understand the motives which inspired me.

I put it as sympathetically as I could when writing to Mr. Norman, pointing out that unless Christmann himself had told it we never should have known; and I was very relieved to receive a reply from him:

What can I say except that you can write to him to explain that having been acquainted with the whole of the circumstances, I now willingly forgive him for the harm he did to my son's memory.

He added a rider that this was conditional on Christmann's allowing the truth to be made known and published in the book I was writing.

I passed on the message with very much thankfulness adding for Christmann's comfort that I did not think it was the way he had given his evidence which had caused all the confusions surrounding the name of "Archambault."

For myself, I thought that even if the book never got published I should have accomplished something in this reconciliation; while in one sense the raking over of these ancient dramas might seem to reopen sores, sometimes my work proved cathartic.

Following up a line of thought which had been developing in my head, I wrote to Christmann concerning a rather delicate matter about which I would really have preferred to speak to him. He had assured me that he had not acted in concert with "Gilbert" in regard to contraband, but did he know anything *about* "Gilbert's" activities in that respect? The affair at Croydon was, of course, post-war; but could Christmann tell me whether it was a frequent thing for agents in the field to become involved in contraband traffic? When a man was active both as an agent and as a contrabandist, did the two *metiérs* run along separate lines or did they tend to become mixed up? He was, I told him, the only person I knew belonging to this world whom I could trust (or for that matter the only person I knew belonging to it), which was the only reason why I asked him. I would be most grateful if he could tell me whether any member of the "French Section", French or British, was engaged in a contraband traffic in gold, platinum, gems or the like. I realised that it was an embarrassing question and, if he did not wish to answer it, I would respect his silence.

In reply I received a letter saying that he knew nothing of "Gilbert's" activity as a contrabandist. He could, however, definitely certify that a certain member of the "Prosper" network (whose name he gave me) had in 1943 been engaged in conducting a contraband traffic in gold and diamonds. They (the *Abwehr*) had, indeed, denounced him to his chiefs in London on this account, as a means of getting him dropped from operations, and he believed that London had in fact responded by relieving him of his post.

He asked me to thank Mr. Norman for his kind words and said he hoped he might be able to see him one day and assure him of the esteem in which he held his son.

As regards the affair at the Square Clignancourt he had done some research into the question of dates. As Sunday, June 6th, his little daughter's birthday, had seen him back in Holland, and the mock arrest of "Anton" at the Restaurant Capucines had taken place on Wednesday and the meeting at the Square Clignancourt on the preceding Thursday, he thought it would be safe to say that this was Thursday, May 27th.

This was very interesting. Christmann thought that his conversation with Kieffer, in the course of which Kieffer admitted to him that "Gilbert" was his agent, had taken place nearly a week or just on a week after the meeting at the Square Clignancourt. Now if one counted forward six days from Thursday, May 27th, it brought one to June 2nd, the date on which "Gilbert" had told the court the Germans first contacted him. It really did look as though he had dated the affair from the moment when it became known outside Kieffer's service. Christmann was *Abwehr*, and seeing the rivalry which existed between the *Abwehr* and the

Sicherheitsdienst, perhaps Kieffer did not feel sure of Christmann's discretion.

Consulting the calendar for 1943 myself, I noticed that June 2nd was a Wednesday, the Wednesday intervening between Sunday, June 6th and Thursday, May 27th. It was also curious that this was apparently the date of "Anton's" mock arrest, though there was probably nothing in the coincidence.

I had for some months been in friendly contact with Dame Irene Ward, D.B.E., M.P. She was engaged in writing a book on the F.A.N.Y. Corps, and since the girls who served in the field were enrolled in the F.A.N.Y. in order to give them a uniform while they were training and a service background, she had come to a good deal of knowledge concerning the organisation of S.O.E. She had followed my researches with a close interest, and was sometimes able to give me curious sidelights on the London angle: for instance that Mr. Attlee, shortly after he took office in 1945, closed S.O.E. down, in despite of pleas that it should be kept on in some form, at such short notice that it had very little time in which to pack up, and that when pressed to explain his decisiveness he said he was 'not going to have a Third International in this country.'

Now she was able to tell me something I had long very much wanted to know; the date on which "Antoine" was parachuted on to the fatal field where he was met by the *Sicherheitsdienst*. "Antoine", really Major Charles Anthelme, a South African descended of an old Mauritian family, was a very important officer, engaged on work more confidential than most of his colleagues in the field knew. During his next to last mission, "Madeleine" had worked in close contact with him, as had Lieut. Garry, chief of the Le Mans or Sarthe sector of the "Prosper" network; and when he returned from France to

London on August 15th, 1943, by the same aircraft as Boddington and some others, it was "Madeleine", over whose radio-circuit all the messages concerning the arrangements were received and sent, and "Gilbert" who saw the aircraft off. When he was later parachuted back again, it was still over "Madeleine's" radio-set that the messages were sent arranging the time and the place and the contacts; only "Madeleine" had been arrested in the meantime and the messages were sent by the Germans and it was they who were waiting to meet him and to bring him as a prisoner to the Avenue Foch. I had long felt it important to know the date on which this happened. Now Dame Irene was able to tell me.

It was February 29th, 1944; Leap Year's Day.

With him on that date had been parachuted a Lieut. Lionel Lee and Miss Madeleine Damerment of the F.A.N.Y. both of whom had been arrested with him as they came down. Miss Damerment, like "Antoine", was dead; she had on September 12th, 1944, been shot at Dachau together with "Madeleine" and two other women belonging to the F.A.N.Y.

The instructions with which these three were sent out from London were that they should on arrival contact "Phono"; "Phono" was the code-name of Garry, and I knew from Ernest that Garry had been arrested on October 18th, 1943, only five days after "Madeleine" who had been arrested on October 13th; this was proof that London had remained unaware of the arrest of both these officers for at least the period elapsed, nearly five months.

There was something here that puzzled me. I had been told by a Madame Jourdan, from whose garden "Madeleine" sometimes transmitted, that in her presence "Madeleine" sent a radio message to London shortly before her arrest, asking to be brought home. I had been told in London that such a message had never been received; yet "Madeleine" had told a number of people that she was returning to London and that an aircraft was being sent to fetch her. She had said her final goodbyes and in one case given a special parting present. Madame Garry had, for her part, told me that she and her husband had been expecting to go to London at the same time as it had been deemed advisable he should consult with the English chiefs; and that as they had thought that they might be kept in England for some months they had been to say goodbye to their relatives. It was indeed in the expectation of finding a message telling them precisely where and when they should go to board the aircraft that was to collect them, that they had gone to the flat the use of which they shared with "Madeleine," unaware that "Madeleine" had just been arrested — arrested in that flat — and that the flat itself was in consequence under surveillance. It was at this flat that they, too, were arrested.

The matter was and remains inexplicable. If "Madeleine" and the Garrys were expected in London, their failure to turn up should have aroused anxiety; and if they were not expected, how had they all got the idea that they were? (I am still able to conceive no theory which does not break down at some point.)

"Gilbert" was in contact both with aircraft and with "Madeleine," though not, so far as is known, with the Garrys. Madame Garry, whom I asked, had never even heard of him; to the best of her knowledge, her husband[45] had contact with London only through "Madeleine" and "Madeleine's" radio. If "Gilbert" had had his hand in this, it would not have been necessary for the Germans to pay to an independent person a very considerable sum of money for the address of the flat used by "Madeleine." Ernest assures me that the arrival of the Garrys at that flat a few days later was unexpected by Kieffer's

---

[45] Garry was hanged at Buchenwald on September 9th, 1944.

service; their capture there was, from the German point of view, a windfall. It was also unknown to Ernest (and he thinks to Kieffer) that "Madeleine" and the Garrys, all three, believed themselves on the point of departure for England. This would put out of court the theory that "Gilbert," who as Air Movements Officer would have known of the operation and been responsible for it if really it had been arranged, had betrayed it to the Germans so that they could arrest the three before they were due to leave; but for Ernest's ignorance, this might have seemed a seductive theory. Ernest, however, had never shielded "Gilbert," and I had no doubt that his ignorance of this intended air operation (if it ever was intended from the London side) was genuine.

If, as I had been told in London, no message asking to be fetched had been received, and no such pick-up operation had been planned, then no message would have been sent to "Gilbert" instructing him to supervise it. But then…?

Any argument upon this theme became circular.

Unable, for the moment, to get further in any direction, I looked again through the copious files which Mr. Norman had left with me. There was a letter from a Madame Renée Guépin expressing her sympathy with his endeavours to clear his son's name from the charges made in the Abbé Guillaume's book, and making a passing reference to "Gilbert," at the time of writing still imprisoned and awaiting trial. Perhaps she knew something significant about "Gilbert"? I flew to Paris on November 21st and asked Mr. Norman to make an appointment with her for me.

After the war, Madame Guépin had been appointed official *Liquidatrice* of the "Prosper" network. In 1943 she had shared responsibility for the Gisors sector. Whilst my researches had not taken me in this direction, I knew that Gisors was one of the spots associated with tragedy. It had been the H.Q. of an Englishman, Captain George Darling, who was after "Archambault" probably the most important of the British officers subordinate to "Prosper". As "Archambault" was a radio operator it was thought by some that Darling would be the more likely "Prospers" successor should anything happen to him. As part of the pact, however, "Prosper" wrote a letter to Darling asking him to surrender to bearer all stocks of arms for which he was responsible. A party of about six Germans, of whom Placke was one, together with some of their French collaborators set off to Gisors where they called on Darling and gave him "Prosper's" letter. As the Germans let a Frenchman do the speaking, Darling seems not to have realised at once that this was a German party and in response to "Prosper's" written instructions led the party in a car (they in their own lorry) to a wood in which one of the dumps was concealed. There an incident caused him suddenly to realise the trap in which he was. He tried to get away in his own car, the Germans fired and hit him and he died the next day in Gisors hospital with Placke watching over him.

Madame Guépin had owned a house in Gisors called *Triechâteau* which Darling had made his H.Q. and where "Prosper" frequently stayed.

Mr. Norman and I went together to see Madame Guépin at her present home in Colombes on November 24th; it was the first time they had met and he had not forewarned her of the real object of the visit and at first spoke mainly of his son, whom he referred to naturally as Gilbert. Then he asked her whom she believed to have betrayed the "Prosper" network.

She started slightly. 'Why — the same name. Gilbert. The other Gilbert. You know that there was another?'

We knew that there was another.

Madame Guépin told us now that on one occasion when "Prosper", "Archambault" and "Denise" had come to stay with her in the latter part of May 1943, an important conversation took place. "Prosper" told them that he did not consider "Gilbert" was to be trusted.

'Did "Prosper" say what he had noticed that had caused him to distrust him?' I asked.

No. He had not said that. He said he suspected "Gilbert" of entertaining relations with the Germans, but he had not specified the ground upon which he suspected him. "Prosper" was the 'big chief' (*le grand chef*) and she did not feel it her part to press him for particulars and she supposed the others felt the same. He would have told them if he had thought it useful. His purpose was purely practical — to warn them that "Gilbert" did not enjoy his confidence and to advise them to be extremely careful in any relations they were obliged to have with him.

She recalled that when "Prosper" told them he did not consider "Gilbert" to be trusted, "Denise" cried out, *'That's what I've been telling you for months!'*

Very soon after this conversation, "Prosper" had told her that he thought it necessary he should go to London to confer with headquarters. She had no doubt whatsoever, and still had none today, that his purpose was to communicate his suspicions concerning "Gilbert." It took a little time to make the arrangements. He had, of course, to leave from one of "Gilbert's" fields, seen off by "Gilbert" himself, since there was no other way of getting back.

When he returned, on June 20th, though he had been away for only ten days, he was a changed man. 'I hardly recognised him,' said Madame Guépin. 'He looked ten years older. He was so grey and strained I thought he must be ill.' She had asked him, and he denied that anything was wrong with him. His appearance was nevertheless so distressing that she could not forbear to press the question. Then he replied: 'It's not my health. It's something much worse. I have not the right to tell you the trouble which is weighing on my mind.' (*'Ce n'est pas ma santé. C'est bien plus grave. Je n'ai pas le droit de vous dire le trouble qui pese sur mon ésprit.'*)

"Gilbert" continued in office. She understood that after the war the British Embassy in Paris had intervened on behalf of "Gilbert" while the French authorities were investigating him.

She must have been the last person to see "Prosper" before his capture, for (in connection with a parachute delivery which had been expected in the area) he spent the night of the 23/24th June at her house at Gisors. He was very overcast.[46] He was catching the 7 a.m. train back to Paris and she accompanied him to the station. He warned her most urgently to look after herself, and she felt he had the presentiment they would not meet again, for after he had said goodbye, he came back twice to say goodbye again. As we knew, he had been arrested at his hotel in Paris immediately on his return, that morning.

She, herself, had not been molested when the Germans came to Gisors for Darling and she supposed that "Prosper" and the others had protected her by making out that she was of no importance. She was not arrested until the new year 1944, through a different affair. In Fresnes, she had been able to snatch a few words with "Denise" who had whispered to her, 'It was "Gilbert" who sold us all' (*'C'est Gilbert qui nous a tous*

---

[46] Marcel Charbonnier who saw "Prosper" at Gisors before he left on the morning of June 24th notified that he 'appeared anxious and urged strict security precautions.' *La Sologne*, p. 77.

vendus'). She had used a soubriquet to distinguish him from "Archambault."

"Denise" had earlier managed to smuggle a note out of Fresnes to her family in which, pathetically, she told them not to worry because 'Gilbert is protecting me' (*'Gilbert me protège'*). Here she must have meant Norman's son whom she loved.

Madame Guépin herself had later been sent to Ravensbrück. She was very frail and obviously delicate, and one realised the toll which these experiences must have taken of her, also that while they had cut into her very deeply she remained deeply loyal to "Prosper."

What did she really think about "Prosper's" last visit to London, I asked her.

There was a moment of ominous silence. "Prosper" had not declared the cause of his increased disquiet on his return, but speculation had been rife in the field. 'At one moment we were all persuaded that the treason came from the top office.' (*'A un certain moment, nous étions tous persuadés que la trahison venait de la boîte même'*).

Who, I asked, was 'we'?

She seemed reluctant to disclose names. Then she said I ought to see a Madame Laure LeBras, whose address she gave me.

The next morning, Friday November 25th, I found my way to the address of Madame LeBras. She was not expecting me, but when I explained that I had her name from Madame Guépin she received me in a very friendly manner.

She was, as she remarked herself, rather older than the other members of the "Prosper" network. She had been recruited into it by a Mademoiselle Germaine Tambour, alias "Annette," who had worked with a French Resistance group which antedated the coming of "Prosper" to France, and which formed one of the original nuclei[47] from which he took over in developing his network.[48] A serious, capable and (in the best sense) a pious woman, Mademoiselle Tambour had remained at all times very close to "Prosper" and had lent him much of her experience in his early days.

On April 20th, 1943, Madame LeBras had had her last conversation with Mademoiselle Tambour. It had been a grave one. Mademoiselle Tambour had told her there was reason to believe that the Germans had regular information concerning their comings and goings, and particularly of the places and times of parachute deliveries. It seemed as if the Germans received intelligence of 'drops' to be made, simultaneously with the members of "Prosper's" network, and she supposed that the code had become known to them.

'Did she say if this came from "Prosper"?' I asked.

Mademoiselle Tambour had not mentioned "Prosper" in this conversation. 'She was not stupid, herself, you understand. But I suppose that she would have been in consultation with "Prosper."'

Mademoiselle Tambour had not indicted anyone in the field. She had said that everything pointed to London. Madame LeBras felt sure that she could give me the exact words Mademoiselle Tambour had used, which she could still hear ringing in her ear. '*La trahison est à la base*,' Mademoiselle

---

[47] Actually a section of the "Carte" network in the south with which Starr had worked in the summer of 1942. After "Carte" went to London a large part of it was taken over by Frager and part by "Prosper." It should be remarked that if the "Prosper" network was the more heavily penetrated by the *Sicherheitsdienst*, the Frager one was the more heavily penetrated by the *Abwehr*.

[48] According to some people Mademoiselle Tambour was actually "Prosper's" first contact on arriving in France.

Tambour had said. *'La trahison vient du départ.'* ('The betrayal comes from the starting-point.')

Madame LeBras would for ever remember this conversation. Only two days later, on the eve of Good Friday, Mademoiselle Tambour was arrested.[49] Her sister, Madeleine, asked to be taken into custody, too, so as to be with her. One year later, to the day, on the eve of Good Friday, 1944, both were sent to the gas chamber at Ravensbrück. The selections for the gas chamber were made in order of physical weakness. This time, it was Madeleine who was selected, and Germaine who asked to accompany her so as not to leave her at the end.

'Forgive me,' Madame LeBras said. 'I cannot help crying whenever I think of it.'

She, herself, had been in Ravensbrück, but did not feel she wanted to speak of it. If I was writing a book, would I put in something about Mademoiselle Tambour, so that her name should not be lost forever? "Prosper" had organised a serious

---

[49] The Abbe Guillaume believes that the arrest of the Tambour sisters should be seen as one of the wave of arrests, all about the same time, proceeding from the penetration of the networks in the south. As an indirect consequence of the arrest in March, 1943, of an agent called Marsac, Peter Churchill and Odette had been picked up on April 16th; the Frager network was next penetrated through the instrumentality of Roger Bardet, who first fell into Bleicher's hands through his association with Marsac, and who was also an associate of both Churchill and Frager. Bardet continued operations on behalf of Bleicher and the *Abwehr* for nearly two years. As Frager's network came to have considerable overlappings with "Prosper's" it cannot be overlooked that there may have been some *Abwehr* penetration of the "Prosper" network from this source. Moreover, the Tambour sisters worked with Marsac and he had their address. As Marsac gave the addresses of about twenty of his colleagues to Bleicher (whilst under a misunderstanding) it is indeed possible they may have been among the victims. See *Colonel Henri's Story* for details of the Marsac affair and of Frager's association through Bardet with Bleicher.

attempt to effect her rescue, but it had failed. (I had heard about this from both the Abbé and Madame Balachowsky who considered that in attempting this rescue he had prejudiced the safety of the rest of the network.)

She would never forget the appearance of "Prosper" during the last days just before his arrest. 'He was always a serious man. But in those last days he trailed the shadow of death before him — in advance, if one can say so.' (*'Il trainait l'ombre de la mort devant lui — d'avance, si l'on peut dire.'*)

She talked to me also of "Denise." Would I put in a word for "Denise"? She did not think the work she had done as a pioneer in the field before "Prosper" and "Archambault" arrived had ever been sufficiently appreciated. She was only twenty-two[50] and to be parachuted ahead of her chiefs to prepare the way for them was a very heavy charge. But she was capable. She had 'a head on her shoulders and a will of iron.' From a *petit bourgeois* family in Boulogne-sur-Seine, Socialist in her ideas, somewhat rough in her manners, she was utterly loyal and devoted to Prosper , as her chief, and to Archambault. I recalled the picture of Denise which Cohen had conjured up: crawling along a rail track on all fours in the darkness and his comment, 'She would derail a train at night and turn up to a rendezvous next morning as though it were all in a day's work.'

The next day, Saturday, I went to the rue Mazagran, a tiny street near the old arch of the Porte Saint Denis, I did not know the name of the hotel but found what I thought must be the right one without much difficulty. The proprietress, Madame Fèvre, was at first not very communicative. Yes, an Englishman had been arrested at the hotel in 1943 but it was nothing to do with them; they had had quite endless visits

---

[50] Born November 18th, 1919.

from the French police and other people asking all manner of questions about it. She had not known that he had anything to do with clandestine activities or even that he was an Englishman. He had registered in the name of François Desprée. (I knew then that I had come to the right place, for that was the name in which "Prosper's" false French identity card had been made out.) He had not been at the hotel more than a day or two, and she knew nothing about him. He had occupied room number 15. Round about 1 a.m. on June 24th a party of Germans had entered and demanded to know which room was occupied by François Desprée. As she gaped at them, too terrified to answer, they seized the register, looked through it, and then all trooped upstairs, presumably to room number 15. There was nobody in it. After a few minutes, some but not all of them came down again and sat to wait with her in her office — she supposed in order to prevent her from warning Monsieur Desprée when he came in — whilst the rest waited upstairs and in other parts of the hotel. They had to wait a long time. The dawn came, and turned to daylight. It was between ten and eleven in the morning that 'Monsieur Desprée' returned and went straight up past the office to his room. A few moments later, he was led down again and taken away by all the Germans together. It was only after the war, when the French police came to question her, that she learned that the man who had been arrested was an Englishman and belonged to the Resistance.

Thus Madame Fèvre confirmed the statement which she had made to the authorities several years earlier. Her evidence seemed to put out of court the story told by "Gilbert," that he had learned at 9 a.m. from "Antoine" that "Prosper" had been arrested at the Café Dupont, Gare St. Lazare. At the same time, since Madame Fèvre said that he had been at the hotel 'only a day or two,' and indeed in as much as he had only returned from London on June 20th, and had spent this night of the 22/23rd at Gisors, he could not have stayed at the hotel more than two nights, it seemed unlikely that this address would have been given in the mail; in any case there would have been no interest to send lodging addresses to London; those in the mail were probably letter-box addresses, from which however people might be trailed. As "Prosper" had become suspicious of "Gilbert" even before his last visit to England, and had asked for Culioli to meet him on his return in place of "Gilbert", it seemed unlikely he would have given him the address of his newest personal lodging. The question how the Germans discovered it remained unanswered.

The next few days were passed in a series of interviews with people who had worked in different Resistance organisations, one person passing me on to another; whilst they gave me material which would have sensation value in quite another case, they did not yield anything concerning "Gilbert" until I came, on December 2nd, to Captain Francis Basin, alias "Olive." He had been the chief of one of the early networks in the south of France which had had a certain amount of contact with "Carte's."

'My position is very delicate,' he said. 'I owe my life to "Gilbert".'

At a certain moment he had been on the run from the Germans; "Gilbert" had put him aboard an aircraft bound for England. 'Well, now, of course I know "Gilbert" was in relation with the Germans. If he had not had an agreement with them he would not have been able to send people off from his fields.' But whatever the nature of that agreement, he was one of those who owed his life to him, if only in virtue of the relations he had established with the Germans. Basin supposed that the Germans, even though they wanted to recapture him, would not have wanted to interrupt a "Gilbert" operation, in case they discredited him with London, and so would not have insisted, once he came under "Gilbert's" wing, even if they knew, "Gilbert" was taking him out of their hands.

This suggested a new way of looking at "Gilbert's" accord with the Germans. I remembered the terms of it as expressed by Ernest: in return for "Gilbert's" keeping them informed of the arrivals and departures and thus enabling them to exercise a surveillance over the agents infiltrated, it was agreed on the German side never to interfere with any of his aircraft or arrest on his field arriving or departing agents. It could indeed be urged that that agreement had enabled him to send off more people to England than would have been possible had he had to hug the shadows in fear of German interception. Against that, unless the Germans had been the gainers in the agreement, why should they have entered into it?

Jerry Morel,[51] said Basin, had sat with "Gilbert" in the plane which fetched him back to England in February 1944; to Jerry, "Gilbert" had acknowledged contact with the Germans but said that it had come about in the effort to save his wife whom they had arrested and threatened to shoot.

This was not the story that was told in court.

He suggested I ought to see Jerry.

I had long wanted to see Jerry Morel but for another reason. I had learned that the man who went out in the plane to speak through the S. phone[52] to the Organiser of the "Canadian" network in the North of France was Jerry Morel; his was the voice that Starr had heard through the listening part of the apparatus and not recognised. Morel had indeed recognised

---

[51] Properly, Major Gerard Morel, usually known as Jerry.
[52] See *The Starr Affair*.

that the voice which spoke from the ground (Von Kapri's) was German, and had on his return reported to Colonel Buckmaster that the network must be considered as German, not Canadian, controlled. This was valuable to me as the confirmation that it was, as Starr believed, his refusal to co-operate by speaking over the S. phone that night, after leading Kieffer to believe until the last moment that he would be willing, which had in fact put an end to Placke's control of the network in the North. A friend of Dame Irene Ward's had tried to persuade Morel to have a talk with me, but he had seemed to think it inadvisable; Yeo-Thomas had also tried, but with no better luck. As he had been a member of the directing staff in London, Morel's position was obviously delicate.

Basin asked me to let him try to persuade Morel to see me; but he was no more successful than his forerunners.

The next day I returned to London.

After that, it was a long time before I learned anything more. On April 23rd, 1956, during another spell in Paris, I saw a little man called Art Watt, known as "Tich," who turned out to have worked closely with "Gilbert" through the winter of 1943, as his radio operator. I asked him what opinion he held concerning him.

'Ah,' he said cautiously, '"Gilbert" is a very controversial personage. Some people are for him and others are against him. He has been much discussed.'

I tried to draw him into taking a position but felt he did not wish to do so. He knew nothing against "Gilbert," he said.

'Did you *like* him?' I asked.

For the first time he was direct. 'Yes,' he said, 'I liked him.' He was an agreeable person to work with; most people in the field were a prey to nerves and anxious forebodings, but

"Gilbert" was always cheerful and never seemed to be worried about anything.

'Did he tell you he was in contact with the Germans?' I asked.

'No. He did not say that.'

I asked him whether he had ever heard him mention "Madeleine." He did not recall it, and did not seem ever to have heard of her.

He had not returned to London until after "Gilbert" and had seen him a day or so before his recall in February. "Gilbert" had met him in a café, and told him he was going and said goodbye.

Watt had, however, more recent news of "Gilbert"; after his acquittal in 1948, Watt told me, "Gilbert" had spent some years in Indo-China flying for a civil airline which plied between different places in the Far East, and as he had a fair knowledge of Chinese or Cantonese had been there doing some job for the French at the time of the siege of Dien Bien Phu. Since then he had returned to France; but Watt did not know whether he was still in France.

I looked in a current Paris telephone directory, and found an entry in "Gilbert's" real name.

I missed Yeo-Thomas in Paris but shortly after my return to England had a letter from him saying he had now interviewed 'well over fifty people' but had been unable to learn anything concerning the case of "Gilbert" beyond what we knew already.

The rest of the year passed without shedding any further light on "Gilbert."

George Adam of the *Figaro Litteraire* was eager to translate the book into French when completed and, early in 1957, suggested that we should, in order to bring matters to a head, make contact both with Major Boddington and with "Gilbert" himself.

This was revolutionary. As regards Boddington, I had written to him twice or three times at an earlier stage in my researches and received no reply; however, I was willing for Adam to try. As for "Gilbert," it had seemed to me useless to call and question him since he would not confirm that he was a traitor. Now, however, I felt that I had been cowardly in not confronting him with the evidence I held against him; I therefore wrote to Adam suggesting that I should come over to Paris and that he and I should see "Gilbert" together: if, indeed, we could persuade "Gilbert" to give us an interview. Adam, however, thought it would be more prudent for him to make the first contact alone.

While Adam and I were discussing by letter the approach to be made, there was a spectacular air crash. A large passenger plane carrying a full complement of passengers had turned over as it landed. The damage, by miraculous fortune or perhaps the skill of the pilot, had been mainly to the aircraft itself, and I received, from Adam and Mr. Norman simultaneously, French newspapers in which pictures of the wreckage were spread right across the front page. Once again, "Gilbert" had hit the headlines. Or rather, an event concerning him had; for this time his name occurred only in small type in a line saying the pilot had been taken to hospital with head injuries.

My first reaction was fear lest "Gilbert" should die; I did not want to find myself attacking a dead man. I briefed my friends to watch the newspapers for any reference to his condition. None appeared. The position was difficult. We knew now for certain where he was, but could hardly take advantage of his being incapacitated in a hospital bed in order to pay him a visit.

It was, in chivalry, an impossible moment at which to face him with charges fourteen years old. We could not know how serious were the injuries he had sustained; he might have only a slight concussion, but decency demanded that the whole affair should be left in suspension for a few weeks before initiating enquiries as to whether he was out and about.

Adam happened to be in contact with Gordon Young of the *Daily Mail* who mentioned to him in a conversation that he had seen Boddington in connection with a book he was writing about "La Chatte." Adam took the opportunity to tell him that he too was anxious to get into touch with Boddington. Shortly afterwards I had a letter from him to say that on March 25th he had received a telephone call from Boddington, saying, 'Gordon Young tells me that you want to see me.'

Adam had then explained to him that he expected to be translating a book concerning certain of the British networks in France during the war, and that as the manuscript contained a good many references to Major Boddington's name he would like to be able to check them with him.

'What is it about exactly?' Boddington had asked.

Adam had replied that it was largely concerned with the development and downfall of the "Prosper" network, and with its consequences.

'Oh, I don't like that at all!' Boddington had exclaimed.

Nevertheless, he had agreed to come to Adam's house at six o'clock the following evening to discuss it.

Adam had waited for him the whole evening, but he had not come; neither had he telephoned nor written to excuse himself.

After that, I authorised Adam to go ahead and make contact with "Gilbert." It was not long before I heard from him again. He had dialled the number given in the telephone directory, and had found himself speaking to "Gilbert" himself. He had explained the matter much as he had to Boddington, and "Gilbert" had agreed to meet him, and "Gilbert" had been as good as his word.

On April 4th they had had quite a long conversation. "Gilbert" was not very sophisticated (*pas très mondain*), wrote Adam; he appeared quite recovered from his recent accident and was apparently resuming flying again. He had already read *Madeleine*; Adam lent him his copy of *The Starr Affair* and told him my new book, resulting from the researches I had made into the downfall of the "Prosper" network, involved him critically. "Gilbert" said he had been tried and acquitted in 1948 and that the matter was closed; if anybody attempted to reopen it upon new grounds (*fait nouveau*), he would bring an action for defamation.

Adam asked whether he would bring the action in England or in France.

If the publication was in England only, "Gilbert" replied, he would shrug his shoulders; but if the book appeared in France he would react violently.

After the war he had been menaced and for a while never went out without a revolver in his pocket; he could put a ball through a jam-jar at thirty paces. Now all he wanted was to be left in peace and not to have his name reinvolved in controversy which could upset his social and business relations; for that reason he would rather not be driven to bring an action for libel and suggested that I might suppress his real name and refer to him simply as "Gilbert."

Adam (who it seemed to me had conducted the interview with extraordinary skill) pointed out that I would be obliged to designate him by the function which he had occupied, and said the best thing would be if he were to meet me so that we could discuss the position and I could tell him the evidence I held against him and intended to publish. "Gilbert" agreed.

I flew to Paris on May 6th and Adam met me at the Air Terminal, with his car. Usually I stayed in an hotel on the Left Bank but, as the triple interview was to take place at Adam's house, high on the Buttes de Montmartre, I had asked him to find me one as near as possible, and we climbed in the car towards the white dome of Sacré Coeur; then across the teeming Boulevard Clichy into the sudden quiet beyond. He had found me an hotel on the corner of the cemetery; after I had dumped my case in my room, which I found had a tranquil view across it, I rejoined him in the car. He and his wife had invited me to dinner, and in the gloaming we pursued a steepening climb into the heart of the village of Montmartre, past the old disused windmill, the *Moulin de la Galette*, and round the bend. His home was in the rue Villa Léandre, a tiny cul-de-sac. One of the almost cottage-style houses a few doors from Adam's had been the headquarters of the *Interalliée* network from which the messages to London had been transmitted, and which had seen the midnight arrest of the Pole who had been co-chief with "La Chatte"; "La Chatte" herself had been picked up by the Germans in the street, one of the narrow cobbled streets which seemed, like most of the 'village', to date from the Middle Ages, only a stone's throw away. All that had been before Adam came to live here. Over dinner we talked over the strategy of the interview to come. Afterwards we came out again and walked towards his car, which he had left parked between his own and that other fateful house, and stood for a moment feeling the silence of the night. We were only just behind the glare of the Boulevard Clichy and the brilliant night-clubs of Pigalle; but here in the 'village' there were few lamp-posts and it was dead quiet.

We looked at the 'other' house, eyeless and blank.

'How close the threads of coincidence draw,' I said to Adam. 'Isn't it strange that the street which played such a part in one drama should see the *dénouement* of another?'

CHAPTER ELEVEN: "GILBERT"

The rendezvous was convened for two-thirty in the afternoon. Adam asked me to come half an hour early, at two o'clock. As I approached the house I noticed a man a little ahead of me on the other side of the road, apparently making in the same direction. Walking more quickly, I overtook and passed him and so it was he who followed me up the steps and stood behind me as I rang the bell. Adam opened the door to find both of us. 'He's followed me up, I think,' I said, looking over my shoulder.

'Oh, no, I haven't followed you!' said "Gilbert," for it was he, as I had supposed. 'Don't begin by thinking bad things!'

'I didn't mean it that way,' I said, not having intended a quip in my opening remark.

Adam introduced us formally and brought us into the sitting-room and, for the first few minutes, made almost the whole of the running of the conversation, both "Gilbert" and I talking only to him, and taking occasional covert looks at each other. He was sturdily built, with tousled fair hair and blue eyes; I judged that he was as embarrassed as I. The conversation ran at first upon unimportant matters, passing from the decor of the room to my books, of which "Gilbert," speaking at last to me, was somewhat critical.

"Gilbert" remarked that he had known Boemelburg in Paris before the war. I had imagined this might be so but had no way of proving it. I had meant to try to obtain an admission by bluff. By declaring it himself in an easy conversational manner he had made it unnecessary.

'Before he became chief of the Gestapo?' I asked. 'While he was attached to the German Embassy in Paris?'

'Yes,' he replied.

The conversation ran on pre-war Paris, and the period of the Phony-war, "Gilbert" now doing most of the talking. I had been reserving my forces but decided that the time had come to close to grips.

'Monsieur, I *know*,' I said.

'Know what?' he asked.

'The real character of your relations with the Germans.'

'Really? Are you an agent or only a writer?'

'I am not an agent. I have made independent researches, but solely for the book I am writing.'

'Then you can't know the whole truth. You are only imagining.'

'I have facts.'

'Don't let us be vague. Give me some details, please. Tell me a precise fact.'

'You were BOE 48.'

'Certainly not. This question has been examined in detail and I have been cleared of it. Everybody knows this except you!'

I offered him a cigarette from my packet as a gesture to establish the humanities but he said he never smoked. I, on the other hand, chain smoked all that afternoon from nervousness.

"Gilbert" continued: 'I don't know who BOE 48 was, but I can swear that it was not me. It was the number of a German agent. God bless me, I have never been a German agent! This was examined for eighteen months running by the British and French secret services. I was declared Not Guilty of any of the charges by a special military tribunal, expert in intelligence affairs. There were twenty-three indictments on the charge sheet and I was acquitted on every one of them. I have had the privilege of military honours and decorations, and I have been promoted since my acquittal to a higher rank, Major,[53] on the reserve list.'

I told him I knew he had been acquitted.

'Then what?' he asked.

'I have discovered facts which were not presented to the tribunal which judged you.' I told him I knew it was he who had handed over the mail of the "Prosper" network to the Germans and that photostats of the same were retained in Kieffer's department at the Avenue Foch.

'But that was examined by the *Juge d'Instruction* and the court. I never went to the Avenue Foch and I never met Kieffer,' he cut in.

'That may be,' I said. 'My informants do not allege that you met Kieffer. It was Goetz who acted as liaison between you and Kieffer.'

'I never met Goetz, except in the office of the *Juge d'Instruction*, and then he made a mistake and picked out the wrong man at an identity parade. And I can tell you he was eager!'

'Ernest was present at your last interview with Goetz, at an empty apartment near the Arc de Triomphe!'

He said that he had never met either Goetz or Ernest. Perhaps this was 'suggested' to Ernest.

'No. He said it to me, and I certainly did not suggest it to him. He could have had no reason to invent such a story.'

'Who knows? It is not for me to imagine the reason. Perhaps he has made a mistake in identification.'

'He recognised your photograph as being that of the man whom he had met in the empty apartment with Goetz.'

---

[53] French Army and Air Force have the same ranks. *Commandant* (Major) is therefore equivalent to Squadron Leader in the R.A.F.

'You put my photograph in front of him and asked him, "This is Gilbert, isn't it?"'

'No. It was after the interview at which he had first told me about you. I was back in England. He was in Germany. I sent him two French newspapers bearing reports of the trial and photographs of you, through the post. It is possible that I asked him if he recognised you — I did not keep a copy of the letter I wrote to him — but I did not put it in such a way as to invite a positive answer. He wrote back freely, saying that he recognised you.'

'It is too easy to "recognise" people that way. Usually the police proceed differently. They mix the man up with others and only then they ask the accuser to say which one he is. If they didn't do this, it would not be fair. They know that otherwise he could make a mistake. Do you follow me?'

I accepted his point about the insufficiency of identification by photograph.[54] I should never have based so heavy a charge on the identification by photograph of a man seen only for ten minutes ten years previously. For me, the fact that Ernest recognised the photograph was only accessory. For one thing, the photograph showed only the face; Ernest had described "Gilbert" to me as almost as tall as himself, and whilst I found it difficult to measure up comparative heights in my mind's eye, "Gilbert" struck me as distinctly shorter than Ernest; and, though he had certainly no spare flesh on him and might be described as wiry, I would have thought he was a little too strongly built to deserve the word 'slender' (*mince*). However, heights and thicknesses, where they cannot be measured by a tape, being in the eye of the beholder rather a matter of

---

[54] "Madeleine" had been mistakenly "identified" in a photograph of somebody else by a member of the "French Section", with resulting distress to her family. See Appendix to Pan Edition.

subjective appreciation, I preferred not to attach too much importance, for the purpose of establishing identity, to the likeness of the physical frame to Ernest's verbal description. It was the internal coherence and quality of his testimony that impressed me. I did not believe that he lied. I felt his seriousness.

'Don't feel too much. And don't accept the fable of the good, poor German lamb, officer of the Gestapo!'

'He had no interest to invent this story, and you have every interest to deny it. I have known Ernest for seven years, and I have never known him tell me anything which was not true.'

Despite this disagreement, the atmosphere was becoming much easier now that we had got down to the subject we were met to discuss. From now onwards, the tone of the long interview, which was to last several hours, was almost throughout friendly, far more friendly than could be imagined from the words used.

He insisted that the whole question of BOE 48 and the mail had been examined already.

I reminded him that Ernest's witness had not been available to the court which tried him; "Gilbert" had been acquitted in 1948 and the French did not get Ernest until 1949. 'One of the *Juges* told him that if they had had his testimony at the trial the verdict might have been different.'

I told him also of the statement Christmann had made me, which showed "Gilbert" to have been in contact with the Germans earlier than June 2nd, the date on which he had told the court he had been arrested and obliged to feign collaboration.

"Gilbert" seemed perplexed and said he thought he had said May 2nd.

'No, you said June 2nd! All the newspapers have got it so it can't have been a misprint. I had to go to considerable pains to establish that you were in fact in contact with the Germans from some time in May.'

He acknowledged freely that the story he had told the court about the two German pilots who had called at his flat on whatever date he had said and asked him to go for a drive with them, and of the men in civilian clothes already in the car, with whom he found himself trapped, should not be taken as factually accurate. He did not, in fact, seem to remember it very well, and it was I who recapitulated it for him as reported by the newspapers. It was, he said, useless for me to examine him on it because it was, to some extent, a conventional presentation. Nevertheless, it was true in the idea if not in the detail. If he had not been trapped in this way and so been obliged to work or feign to work for the Germans, he had in fact known two German pilots before the war and come across them again during the period of his mission; and if his first contact with the German services had not come about through this it really did not matter. To tell the whole truth would have been too complicated, too long, and would have involved revealing too many things. It had been necessary to make a simplification and to present something short and easily comprehensible.

At this juncture Adam said he would go and fetch some beer, and left us.

'But why did Boddington say what he did?' I asked.

'Didn't he say he had been present in the room at the War Office when I was briefed to approach the Germans on my return to France?' enquired "Gilbert," somewhat uncertainly.

'No, he didn't. He supported the story you had just told the court. He said you told him about it when he arrived in France in July.'

'Oh, yes, that was it. Of course! I remember now.'

'But then why did he say it?'

'I don't know. Probably he said what was appropriate to the circumstances.'

'If your evidence was partly untrue, why did Boddington go into the box to confirm it?' I asked brutally.

'He thought it was the truth. I did not suggest it to him and I did not press him. He did it spontaneously, at least so far as I was concerned. Boddington was not questioned in court about the way I got into contact with the Germans or they with me.'

He would rather not say anything about Boddington; I must please not press him.

'But that is the knot of the problem!'

'Yes,' he said simply. 'That is the knot of the problem.'

'But what is the knot?' I urged. 'Why did Boddington do it?'

'That you should ask Boddington,' he said.

I told him Adam had invited Boddington to come and see him but that he had failed to turn up. 'Can't you tell me, since we can't get hold of him?'

He shook his head. It would not be permissible.

I felt I had to respect this, and did not press further.

A few minutes earlier he had still been maintaining that he had, all the same, been authorised by somebody on behalf of the "French Section" to maintain contact with the Germans. Now suddenly he said, 'Very well, I was not authorised...'

I was just heaving a sigh of relief, thinking that I had obtained an admission, when he added, 'Not by the "French Section." By another organisation in London.' I thought he had at first meant the first part of the sentence to stand by itself, and had covered himself by a second thought.

Adam came back with the beer and I exclaimed, 'We have made some progress while you have been out!' And told him what had passed.

'I expressed myself badly,' said "Gilbert," mischievously. 'It was not by the "French Section" that I was authorised, but it was by London all the same. Some of my chiefs were for me, others against me. London at one moment did not trust me. I was not really authorised, for a moment, because the whole thing had got too big and too desperate. For a time I had to carry on without being really authorised, but I succeeded and then everybody was on my side.' With regard to the inexactitude of the evidence he had given, he maintained the details concerning the manner in which he had first come into contact with the Germans were of little interest compared with what had been achieved.

I noticed that he seemed to be more distressed by questions concerning Boddington's evidence than his own, and I felt he did not want us to attack Boddington. Perhaps he felt gratitude towards him. It was the first likeable trait he had shown.

'I have some consideration for *you*,' said Adam, 'since you have come here, but I am under no obligation to *him*.'

'If you're concerned about him, it's for you to contact him and bring him here,' I suggested.

He shook his head; he had not been in communication with Boddington for years.

'Can't you write a story about Tarzan or Jumbo?' he asked (not directly in connection with this but soon after), 'instead of putting your nose into this stinking business.'

I said it was precisely to get at the truth of this 'stinking business' that interested me.

'It is too recent to tell the whole truth. Some people are still alive or even on duty. Come back in fifty years and I'll tell you the truth!'

'I know it already.'

'What?'

'That you were BOE 48.'

'*Encore!*'

He repudiated this as before and there followed a long wrangle; he declared again that this was the number of another person who had done the things with which I charged him.

Adam pressed him to give some details about this other person.

'I'm very sorry,' he said, 'but I must not interfere with the action of another agent, even if it makes my position look awkward to you.'

I told him I did not believe in his pose of chivalry, and reminded him of the depositions he had made against "Prosper" and "Archambault." 'You accuse everybody, when it suits you!'

He said he had not accused them; Adam opened a copy of the Abbé's book in front of him and showed him extracts from his own depositions.

Well, he said, he had been referring only to the pact, which was common knowledge.

He said BOE 48 had been another man, also called "Gilbert."

Inspired, I knew, by generous motives, Adam kept questioning him about this other Gilbert. 'Can't you give me some idea what he was like? A physical description if not his name. Because everything turns on the existence of this other man. It is all your honour or all his.'

Cutting in, I said to Adam, 'There isn't any other. It's him.'

'But I would like to believe him that there is another, if he can convince me.' And he sought again to draw "Gilbert" out on this subject.

"Gilbert" fell back upon the position that his lips were closed. 'I can say nothing. I am forever prisoner of the job I did. I have sworn not to reveal secret matters and I keep my oath.'

'You are an eel!' I said.

'Thanks for the compliment. Don't forget that I have been an agent. A good agent.' At another moment he said, 'Orders are orders.'

'Don't try to make me believe that you are still under orders and still an agent.'

'Certainly not. Now I am *brulé* in every country. That keeps me out of temptation and prevents me from dying young. I am only forty-seven. I can't even look too long at a pre-war car without having a cop in my back saying, "Move on, sir, move on."' But as regards the past, orders were still binding upon him, he said.

At another moment, when he was being particularly eellike, I exclaimed, 'You know all the ways of getting yourself out of things!'

'I have an interest!' he retorted disarmingly.

'Look,' I said. 'You have been acquitted and nobody can do anything to you.'

'It is so,' he said.

'So it can't hurt you to tell us the truth now and avow that it was you.'

'He can't avow it if perhaps it wasn't.' Adam put in gently.

'It was him,' I said, implacably.

The argument threatened to become circular again.

"Gilbert" turned to the "Prosper" network itself, saying that it had been penetrated from a very early stage and from more than one side. This I was bound to agree, for I knew it. I was prepared even to agree when he declared that the nucleus from which it grew had been penetrated before "Prosper" ever arrived on the scene.

I was thinking of the "La Chatte" drama and of the fact that not only she but some of her former agents went over to Borchers and his subordinate, Bleicher; and also of Bleicher's statement that he was, later, through his agent, the traitor Roger Bardet, in contact with "Denise" and some of her colleagues, for whom the *Abwehr* issued identity cards of which they kept copies on their own files. I knew also that between the "Prosper" and Frager networks there were considerable inter-connections and that Roger Bardet was Frager's right-hand man, through whom the secrets of the Frager network and others with which it came in contact were regularly betrayed to the Germans.

"Gilbert" declared, "'Prosper' picked agents from Frager who had picked some from "Carte" and from "Noble 1,"[55] where "La Chatte" was, and in all of these networks there were already German agents. He spoke of the attempt made by "Prosper" to rescue the Tambour sisters, and declared that in paying a bribe to the *Abwehr* officer who was to supervise their transport from one prison to another[56] he laid himself open to

---

[55] George Noble, one of the earliest agents of the "French Section" to be sent into the field. In 1941 he worked as radio organiser to Pierre de Vomécourt, who was later introduced to 'La Ghatte' after she come under German control.

[56] The arrangement was that the official in charge of the Black Maria was to stop it by the roadside and hand the two sisters over to "Prosper's" men. The Black Maria stopped all right and two women were handed out but they were the wrong ones, nothing to do with

being trailed. I had heard allusions to this, and the same criticism made in respect of it, by both Madame Balachowsky and the Abbé, so made no reply. But when he spoke of the pact, I declared: 'The pact was an epiphenomenon. They concluded the pact because they knew they had been betrayed, and it is not for you to speak of that!'

'It is not an excuse and I have my idea which is quite different,' "Gilbert" said violently.

He said amongst other things that "Prosper" had tried to annex him under his command.

'But "Prosper" was in the field months before you were,' I said, meaning that "Prosper" would be his natural senior.

'I asked London what to do,' he continued, ignoring the interruption, 'and the answer was "Cut at once, you are your own chief in the field."'

'Did you warn him of the German infiltration?'

'Not really,' he said; but he had criticised his action in respect of the Tambour sisters.

'Did you tell him you were in contact with the Germans yourself?'

'No,' he said simply enough; he had thought it better not to do that.

'In May "Prosper" expressed to someone his suspicion that you were in contact with the Germans. If you had told him yourself, he would not have been left to form suspicions.'

'I know, but anyway when he went to London in June he was seen off by myself from one of my fields. If he was suspicious of me, why did he let himself be seen off by me?' He said "Prosper" had had to spend three days with him at Amboise while waiting for the aircraft.

"Prosper's" network.

'He didn't like having to do it. But there was no other means of getting to London.'

He shrugged.

'Nuts! There were M.T.B.s, submarines and the route through Spain. Do you imagine "Prosper" stupid enough to throw himself into the lion's mouth? No, he knew that with me he was taking no risk and that my pick-up operations were always successful, for I never missed. It was hard enough work to be excused being proud of.'

He made allegations against a number of other members of the "Prosper" network, and I would not listen to his blackening his colleagues.

'But I don't blacken them,' he said. 'Spying is not a business for angels. It is only to people who do not understand this that some of the shifts to which I refer would look black.' He wanted to say that some of the people whose names occurred in my books had put their foot in it one way or another, but he did not mean, by saying that, to blacken them.

'They were perhaps not without fault,' I allowed, 'but you are not the person to say it. You are the last person to be in a position to make criticisms of "Prosper" or of anybody.'

"Gilbert" answered, 'Listen, Miss Fuller. "Prosper" was magnificent, strong, young, courageous and decisive, a kind of Ivanhoe; but he should have been a cavalry officer, not a spy. He was not sufficiently trained in these things. In Great Britain we learned how to jump by parachute, to use all kinds of arms, open any lock, write in code, use wireless and so on. But nobody can teach reckless people to be calm and to weigh things carefully; it is no more possible than to teach audacity and decisiveness to the overprudent.'

'That may be,' I said, 'but we are getting away from the subject. It is not "Prosper" whom we are met to discuss but you.'

'Well then?'

'I should like to tell you what I honestly believe,' I said. 'I have always believed that you knew something against the people in London, and that they were in your hands in consequence and were obliged to protect you for fear you would tell what you knew about them.'

I thought this might sound offensive, and was really surprised when he replied in the simplest manner, and with a radiating smile, 'But of course! That's exactly it! But not in the bad sense. In the sense of discretion only, not complicity. A tacit accord. It's elementary.'

I told him this interested me very much, and that I had from the beginning seen him as a 'pointing arrow.'

This seemed new to him. 'Do you mean that you saw me as something leading to something else?' he asked.

'Yes. What is significant in your case is that the English protected you, knowing you to be guilty.'

He reacted for the first time with anger. 'I am not guilty. I have proved it and I can still prove it even after the deposition of Ernest.'

'Yes, you are guilty!'

'No, I am not guilty!'

'Yes!'

'No!'

'Yes!'

'No!'

Tension was mounting with these repetitions, which threatened to become childish.

'Yes!' I said again.

He looked me deep in the eyes, and said with a smile, 'If you believe it.'

'I do,' I said quietly.

He shrugged slightly, still smiling.

There were lighter moments after that, as when he said, 'You must never believe me further than you wish, Mademoiselle, for I can't always tell the whole truth.' This I found almost touching.

At one moment I told him that I did not accuse him of lacking courage.

'Nobody could,' he said, and spoke of his service in the R.A.F. and how he had been shot down by the Germans in September, 1944, and badly hurt.

I told him I knew of his service in the R.A.F. and was not trying to take that away from him. But that did not affect the charges I made.

As the discussion progressed through detailed intricacies, he seemed for a moment to think I was accusing him of complicity in all manner of different episodes with which to the best of my knowledge he had, in fact, no connection.

'No,' I said. 'There is really only one thing that I reproach you. That you gave the mail entrusted to you by "Prosper" and "Archambault" to the Germans, and so were responsible for their arrest.' (I had for the moment forgotten the field at Angers, of which however I spoke to him later.)

He denied again vehemently that he had handed over the mail, or that he was BOE 48, and said that I did not show him the proofs.

'But I do show you the proofs,' I said. And I told him for the third or fourth time what Ernest had said. He said that still left room for confusion and that I had not shown proof that the person referred to was him.

'Let me establish the chain for you,' I said. 'It is a fact that they had at the Avenue Foch photostats of the Prosper mail bearing this number. After Boemelburg went to Vichy and bequeathed you, so to speak, to Kieffer, you became for Kieffer's service as for the French Section simply Gilbert.' The reference number was no longer needed since they now had you directly. Now Goetz became your contact and acted as liaison between you and Kieffer. Now that you had become a person to them and not just a number, Ernest would hear of you sometimes from Kieffer and sometimes from Goetz, and he always knew that you were the old BOE 48 whom they now called simply Gilbert. The reference number was no longer and Kieffer did not like the idea of Goetz going to meet you alone as usual, in case you had the idea of kidnapping him or something, and so he told Ernest to go too. He went with Goetz to the empty apartment of which Goetz had the key, and there you met them. You confirmed that you were going, gave them the B.B.C. message that would announce your safe arrival in London and told them that one "Marc" would be your successor in the field. You were recalled in February.

'February 4th,' he put in; and revealing a taste for precision he added that London had asked him to return on the 1st, that he had found that impractical and replied that he would return not on the 1st but on the 4th and that on the 4th he had indeed returned.

'So the date makes it you. And Ernest recognised your photograph in the French papers I sent him, reporting your trial. He said he recognised the man he had met with Goetz in the empty flat. But in any case, without that, the date of the recall makes it you.'

He said all this was fantasy.

'But you can't escape that chain.'

He said some facts in that chain were true but he was not BOE 48.

'But I have just *proved* it to you,' I said, exasperated.

'For *you* it is proved,' he said with a smile.

'It is proved,' I said.

He refused to accept Ernest's testimony.

'But I *know* it is true.'

'It is true for *you*,' he said, giving me a very deep look, and a smile with it. 'If you believe it.'

He spoke about "Madeleine" and he said he had known her quite well.[57] He had been amused to see in my book references to mysterious unnamed men who would call at the Boulevard Richard Wallace to collect packets which she would leave with the concierge for them to pick up. 'They came from me,' he said. 'I sent them.'

'The concierge didn't know who they were. I only had this information from the concierge.'

'I could have told you all about it. Why didn't you come to me when you were writing the book?'

'I had never heard of you!'

He seemed really surprised.

'I never even suspected your existence,' I told him. I had never even heard him mentioned by the authorities in London either as "Gilbert" or by his real name, and that I had not even known there was a special person charged with arrangements for the reception and despatch of aircraft. 'It was only in 1954 that I heard your name.'

'In 1954!' He seemed quite amazed.

'From Ernest. It was he who told me.'

---

[57] Much later he told me it was he who received her when she was landed in France by Lysander on June 16th 1943.

I pointed out that I had had to pick up my knowledge of the "French Section" as I went along. 'Nobody in London to this day has ever spoken your name to me. You aren't mentioned in Colonel Buckmaster's book[58] and to speak to the people in London one wouldn't know such a person as you had ever existed. I think that for them you are a skeleton in the cupboard!'

He seemed intrigued and amused by this.

Reverting to "Madeleine", he said that she and "Antoine" had travelled down with him on the same train from Paris to Angers where they were to wait for an aircraft to pick them up by the light of the July moon. He kept them both under the same roof as himself in a country place and had Robert Benoist, who was also with them, put up nearby. They had to wait three nights as on account of bad weather the operation was first postponed then cancelled for that moon. He dismissed all three with appointments for the next moon. They were evidently at a loose end and Robert Benoist invited "Madeleine" and "Antoine" to come back with him and be his guests at his home in Auffargis at any rate for a few days. He saw "Antoine" again on August 16th when the operation was laid on again and he saw him off with Boddington and others; but this time "Madeleine" was not of the party; he did not think it his business to ask about her and did not see her again.

'Oh yes you did!' I exclaimed. 'You must have seen her at least once more because you submitted to the Germans the report written by Andrès which "Madeleine" gave you to send to London by aircraft. That report was about the bombing of

---

[58] I was of course referring to his first book *Specially Employed*. But his new book *They Fought Alone* likewise contains no reference to "Gilbert"; more remarkable, it contains no references to Major Boddington, his second in command who is even omitted from his tabulation on p. 74 of his staff at H.Q.

Boulogne-sur-Seine and Courbevoie which took place in the middle of September, so you must have seen her at least at late as then.'

He said he had not given the Germans a report from "Madeleine."

I told him Madame Aigrain had told me she had given Andrès' report to "Madeleine", that "Madeleine" told her she had given it to "Gilbert", and that after Madame Aigrain's own arrest a couple of months later she was shown a photostat of the report at the Avenue Foch.

He disputed hotly this circumstantial evidence.

'It is confirmed by Ernest,' I said. 'He remembered the report well; Kieffer told him to confront "Madeleine" with it, and afterwards he showed it to both Madame Aigrain and Andrès. That shows he knew the chain of hands through which it had come to reach them.'

"Gilbert" refused to be convinced that it was he who had handed it to the Germans for photostatting, and repeated that he had not seen "Madeleine" up to so late a date.

'What did you think had happened to her?'

He had not really thought about it; he had just lost sight of her.

I told him the story of the mysterious message asking to be fetched home which "Madeleine" sent to London by radio, according to Madame Jourdan, but which the authorities in London said they had never received; and of the conviction shared by "Madeleine" and the Garrys which they communicated to several people, that an aircraft had in fact been laid on for them in October. 'If such arrangements had really been made you would have been responsible for them.'

He said he knew nothing about any of this. 'But "Madeleine" had been trailed for at least a month and I suppose that the radio game had already started. Even the Germans operating from Paris could have answered the message of "Madeleine" in such a way that she would think it was London replying.'

The idea that reply messages could have been sent to "Madeleine" from an unauthorised operator, had her wavelength somehow become known, was to me a new one; yet against the theory that such a pirate transmission might have emanated from Kieffer's department was Ernest's obvious ignorance of it.

The mystery remained as deep as ever.

I admitted that, since London said the message was never received, perhaps no arrangements had in fact been made for an aircraft to be sent. But "Madeleine" had said goodbye to so many people that it was difficult not to think there had been a misunderstanding, and if there had been an aircraft sent to pick her up then he, "Gilbert", must have known that she was not there to get into it.

'You're not trying to accuse me of complicity in the arrest of "Madeleine" are you?' he cried.

'No. Because I know how that happened and that it was nothing to do with you.'[59] But it was, I maintained, difficult for me to believe that he did not know that she had been arrested.

It was not the kind of interview in which one deals methodically with one subject at a time; we looped back continually to ground which we had previously crossed. So we came back to Christmann.

'What did Christmann say exactly?' he asked.

---

[59] "Madeleine" had been arrested as the result of a denunciation; the circumstances of the case gave no cause to doubt that it was a spontaneous act and there was no reason to suppose the person who made it to have had any relations with "Gilbert."

I told him again, with all the detail I could remember, and he listened attentively. When I came to the point that when they were confronted by the French authorities after the war Christmann recognised in him a man whom he had seen at the Avenue Foch, "Gilbert" protested.

'Christmann lies on that point. I was never at the Avenue Foch.'

'I was surprised myself because Ernest told me he had never seen you at the Avenue Foch, but I don't think Christmann would have invented this.' I told him how, so far from wanting to make trouble for him, Christmann had told me what he knew of him with reluctance and put in a very strong plea for charity. 'He has a sentiment for you because he thinks he sees in you something the same kind of man that he is himself.'

"Gilbert" made a movement of slight impatience.

'He kept silent in front of the French, which was not in his interest since he was, himself, a prisoner,' I pointed out. 'He even went so far as to charge Gilbert Norman in order to cover you. It was only because he felt he had done a wrong to the family, when I put that to him, that he told me the truth and authorised me to publish it. It was not from spite against you and he felt rather bad about it because you had given him a present out of gratitude for the cover he had given you.'

'I did not give Christmann any present.'

'It wasn't a bribe. He made that clear. He did what he did spontaneously and without ulterior motive. A small present reached him in his cell afterwards, but he hadn't been expecting it.'

'I never gave him any present!'

'As a matter of fact, he had no proof that it was from you. There was a piece of paper inside with just one word written on it in block capitals: MERCI. He couldn't think of anybody else who would have a reason to thank him and so he supposed it was you.'

Perhaps he had done a favour for somebody else and forgotten about it, "Gilbert" suggested.

At one moment he declared, 'The Germans in Paris had higher orders to respect me. If I had betrayed "Prosper" to them they wouldn't have liked that. They wouldn't have thought well of me. And they did.'

'I can't let you get away with that!' I exclaimed. 'I can tell you one, at any rate, who didn't!'

'Who?'

'Kieffer.'

'Kieffer's dead!'

'I have his words from Ernest. Do you want to know what he said about you? It's not nice. Do you want to hear it?'

There was just a slight hesitation. Then he said in a small voice 'Yes.' He looked me straight in the eyes and I could feel he was bracing himself to take it.

'He said: "He betrays the English and his own compatriots to us; he would betray us to them the day it suited him better."'

A silence for a moment or two. '*Eh bien*,' he said quietly. 'Ah well!'

I wished he smoked; for I would have liked to offer him something.

'Kieffer didn't know me,' he said, breaking the silence. 'Perhaps if he had known me, he wouldn't have said that.'

He thought that the Germans with whom he had direct relations appreciated that he would not give them information enabling them to make an arrest.

'But you did!' I said.

He repudiated it, and we were back on the old roundabout.

As we talked on about the problems of agents in the field he said that at one time he had had to carry on without instructions, and that when one was without instructions one had to make decisions on one's own responsibility and perhaps even to make sacrifices, and afterwards it might be that one would be blamed for what one had taken on oneself.

'Are you trying to say that you were authorised but that you went too far?' I asked him.

'I scarcely know what answer I can make to this. But I never sacrificed anybody. All my agents are still alive. In all my operations I took the most dangerous part. Some I did alone even, with absolutely no aid because it was too dangerous. It is impossible nowadays to imagine what it was like.'

Again, he said, one should distinguish between those who had betrayed their colleagues from interest, that was to say for money, and those who did so only to save their lives.

I pounced on this, though — as I was almost beginning to feel sorry for him — as delicately as possible. 'You have already told us you were not under duress, so I can only suppose you did it from interest.'

For the second time there was anger. 'I did not take money!' Then, after a pause, 'Not much. Not what I call money. Not substantial.'

Strangely enough, I believed the latter part of this answer. The voice in which he pronounced the modifying phrases rang true, and convinced me, for myself, that money, even though it had been accepted, had not been the motive. There was something here that I did not understand, but I felt some honesty at this moment and in consequence more respect.

"Gilbert" explained his meaning further. 'It was not dirty money. First, as I was not a German agent, I did not receive a monthly salary. It is well known, because we have the pay-list of both Gestapo and *Abwehr* agents. Secondly, as I never gave people or anything to the German services I was not in a position to get a reward for it. Thirdly, on my job it would have been stupid to take any, as it would have caused me to be distrusted. But I had the possibility to make some personal profit on some international business in which German as well as British businessmen were involved. And they took the best part, leaving me only the crumbs!'

As an afterthought he added, 'As Christmann told you smuggling business and spying are cousins.'

"Gilbert" besought me, 'Remember what you have heard already from so many people, that there were supposed to be German agents in London, in this cosmopolitan organisation. We agents, working in occupied countries, living on our nerves, were open to tales. Some thought only, some had what they called proofs, some ventured names — some knew. For these, tales were not tales. But for these it was worst. All of us had the weight of this on the chest, like a stone. We avoided reporting to London, because of this. I took' my own measures 'without knowing at the beginning that they were in line with what London wished; but it took time before my chiefs in London recognised that I had puzzled the Germans in Paris, and what was more, the Germans in London also.'

I asked him if he would give me some details by which I might check his assertion concerning the existence of German agents in London, but he would not. He had spoken of this only to explain that without being a prisoner, one could be the prisoner of a *situation*, which was much worse.

Reaching out to him now, I said, 'You must realise that I am being nice with you. You must appreciate that I am being nice with you.'

'Yes,' he said. 'But, for my part, I could have reacted to this in a nastier way than I have.'

'I appreciate that, too,' I said.

He said that all that concerned him really was that his real name should not appear. He had his present job, and he had his house in the country and his garden, and he did not want his life turned upside down. 'Say "Gilbert", and say all the bad things you like,' he said.

'I will,' I said.

When first I asked him what he had against London, he had said he could not tell me. He protested, too. I have nothing against London. The word is too crude. Can't we, agents between ourselves, keep a secret? That isn't blackmail. Later, when I spoke of the radio-game and said I could not understand how they did not know in London that "Archambault" had been arrested, seeing that "Madeleine" and others had transmitted news of his arrest, "Gilbert" exploded, saying that of course they knew. He, too, had told them. He remembered the telegram he had received from London, *Qui a sauté?* Who has been arrested?) He replied with a list, "Prosper", "Denise" and "Archambault" were on it, he was sure. 'I reported to *one* of my chiefs that I had *seen* "Archambault" and "Denise" led out of the house 51 rue des Petites Ecuries where "Denise" had her apartment in handcuffs.[60] On that occasion the Germans shot at me. Curious, isn't it?'

We spoke about Starr's theory that the radio-game had been kept up deliberately from London, and that men had been sent

---

[60] Actually, "Denise" had been arrested together with "Archambault" at the Laurents, but it seems the Germans afterwards took them both with them to call in at "Denise's" probably to collect some things she had left in her own place.

out without being warned that they were being deliberately sacrificed for the sake of keeping it up.

'The ways of H.Q. are impenetrable,' said "Gilbert."

'But what would be the purpose of keeping it up?' I asked. 'It does not seem that it was used for the dissemination of false intelligence to the enemy.'

'It was rather to keep the Germans occupied. To distract their attention, I think.'

I drew a breath, for this was exactly Starr's theory, which he had written in his report on returning to London in 1945. 'You believe, then, that the whole "French Section" was sacrificed?'

'My theory — I won't tell it to you — is not so crude as yours. I knew, and I reported on my visit in Easter 1943 to London, that the "French Section" was penetrated from a very early stage, from before "Prosper" was even parachuted into the field. I suppose "Prosper's" chiefs knew that and that they handled it in their own way.'

I could not understand what he was driving at. Then we discussed the possibility that a decision might have been taken to write the whole thing off, in the real sense, and yet to allow it to continue in order to give the Germans something to handle and to occupy their attention, and so to protect another British organisation in France which had been launched upon a different and more serious basis. The "French Section" would, in this case, have become nothing but a cover for this. (I thought of "Prosper's" visit to London in June and wondered whether this was what he had sensed.)

'But if the Section was used like this, do you think Colonel Buckmaster knew?'

'I don't think so. As for me, I reported to an officer of much higher rank, and I believe that Buckmaster did not know at that time.'

We fell silent for a moment.

'Have you met Gubbins?' he asked suddenly.

'No.'

'It's a pity,' he said. I cannot recall with certainty the words he used in speaking of Major General Gubbins, but it was less the words than the tone which impressed me by its seriousness, and the respect with which he pronounced this name. It was the more remarkable because respect of persons was not his outstanding characteristic. But one of the few certainties that were to remain with me after this interview was that he genuinely respected Gubbins.

He did not, however, believe that it was from within S.O.E. that the decision to make a manoeuvre, of the kind he was inclined to credit, had been taken.

'Where was it taken, then?'

He could not say. He supposed in another quarter.

'And the people in this other quarter, were they animated by honest motives or dishonest?'

'Honest!' he said, and for a moment the eyes were blazing. That was another moment that was to remain with me, and to give me long pause for thought.

The tone in which we were talking had changed considerably; during these minutes he had been speaking seriously and without exaggeration. Whilst disbelieving what he said in attempts to clear himself, I believed him in what he said in these minutes; that is, I believed that he himself genuinely believed that a strategic sacrifice had been planned from London.

He had, he said, come to a personal conviction about this in the course of the visit he paid to London in Easter 1943, and had thereafter on his return to France taken his own measures. I thought of the strange forebodings which "Prosper" had conceived in his mind during *his* visit to London (only six weeks later, for he went in June), though he had gone to London already suspecting "Gilbert." The thought occurred to me that if only "Gilbert" could, after his visit at Easter, have confided in "Prosper" instead of 'taking his own measures' a tragedy might have been averted.

In order to be certain, I asked "Gilbert" what he meant when he said that he had on his return to France 'taken his own measures.'

'I managed to get myself solicited by a German agent — on my own initiative in the first place — but soon I informed my chiefs of the steps I had taken. I went secretly once more to London. There I received the order to carry on my mission of Air Movements Officer and "*other*" orders also.'[61]

He could reveal nothing more of his instructions, except that they related to the Intelligence side. He appreciated that it was impossible for us to check what he said; but it was impossible for him to help us in this sense.

It was getting late and the light was beginning to fade. He said he must go and rose to do so. Suddenly I remembered the Bony and Lafont depositions accusing Starr.

'I must tackle you about this! Sit down!' I put my hands on his shoulders and almost sat him down by force. 'Those depositions were on the *Dossier "Gilbert"*.'

He started to object, then said, 'Well I suppose they would have been. I hadn't thought about it.'

'They made it look as though Starr had been responsible for the downfall of the "Prosper" network and they were false. Why did they write them?'

---

[61] This was afterwards written out by "Gilbert" himself, by hand, in English.

'I don't know,' he protested, laughing despite himself. 'I didn't inspire them! I was in hospital during the time they were being examined. I was shot down on September 9th, 1944.'

I accepted that, for I knew that he had been shot down soon after he went back into the Air Force. 'I wasn't supposing that you would have been able to visit them in their cells, anyway. But those depositions attached to your file could only have appeared as evidence for your defence. If Starr had been responsible there would have been less reason to suspect you and it looks as though somebody were concerned to shield you.'

'I can't help it,' he pleaded, still laughing. 'I don't know anything about it. Can I go now?'

I let him get up, but we stood for quite a while afterwards talking about this and that.

His reference to having rejoined the Air Force after release from S.O.E. reminded me of the line in *Combat* saying that "Gilbert" had, following his recall from the field to London in February, 1944, been placed under arrest and held in custody for a period of sixty days ending September 1st. I had supposed he had been kept in Brixton prison, but thought now that I should check this with him.

'I was not under arrest, I was distrusted,' he said. He had, for the purpose of interrogation, been detained, but not in a prison. He was ordered first to The Swan Hotel, Stratford-on-Avon, and then to the Savoy Hotel, London. Here he remained for some time with only minor restrictions on his liberty (i.e. he had to undertake not to speak with any of the French) and became quite attached to the sights and sounds of the river. Shortly after D-Day, he was notified that he was free to leave the Savoy if he wished and he returned to his own London flat. Finally he was allowed to rejoin the R.A.F. He was shot down on September 9th while strafing a retreating German and unable to bale out crashed with one wing left and had eight months in bed.

There was only one further moment of friction between us; that was when he again made adverse comments on other members of the "Prosper" network.

'Don't say anything against anybody!' I interrupted. 'It only repels me!'

'For hours *you* have been saying the *most* disagreeable things to *me*,' he retorted.

I had to admit the retort was justified. I had talked to him straight; he had received my attacks with courtesy and had at no time retaliated. By that, at least, I was impressed.

By this time we were all three tired, so it was agreed that I should write out a *compte rendu* of the interview and give him a copy so that he could see that it had been done honestly. Once more he formally denied all the charges I had made against him and affirmed that there had been a mistake in identification.

'You know that I don't believe you,' I said.

'And you know that I don't mind,' he said. 'It doesn't matter to me.'

'I don't want your head!' I said.

'You couldn't get it,' came his repartee.

But we were both smiling as we shook hands.

Just at the door, he turned again and said, much more seriously, 'It is too recent. If we were all dead it would be different. It isn't possible at this time to tell the whole truth. In fifty years!'

And he was gone down the path.

My watch had stopped. Adam looked at his. It said a quarter to eight. He had been with us for nearly six hours. Left to ourselves, we paced the room for a bit but were too exhausted to attempt much in the way of analysis of what had passed. I went back to my hotel and spent most of the night writing out as close a record as I could of the conversation which had taken place, in a sense more for my own future reference than for publication as it stood; I realised that cuts would have to be made but wanted to get it down on paper while the actual phrases used were still fresh in my memory.

The next day I took it round to show Adam.

'Well, what do you think of him?' he asked me.

'The dreadful thing is — I like him!'

'So do I! But he told us a magnificent cover story and threw in a few grains of truth to catch our attention and make us swallow a great quantity of lies.'

The great quantity of lies could scarcely be a matter for dispute; the difficulty was how to select from among them the grains of truth. One could make a bad selection and reject what one should retain as easily as the reverse. I was baffled by something of a different order.

'I don't understand why I am not repelled by his personality. Because I am very quick to react from anything foul. And I know he did these things.'

'You are quite sure of that?'

'I know Ernest's testimony is genuine. Ernest is in good faith.' This was the real ground on which I stood.

'You are quite sure that it is him and not some other man?'

'I know that it's him.'

'There is no consciousness of guilt there,' said Adam. 'That's why one feels the personality as sympathetic.' After a moment's reflection, he said, 'Amoral. Not immoral. Amoral. You understand me?' His idea was that the reason why one did not feel the presence of a bad conscience was that there was no conscience at all.

For me that presented a philosophical difficulty; for me, a human being was almost by definition a being endowed with a conscience, for which reason I have never taken easily to the doctrine of diminished responsibility.

For my part, I could not attempt an explanation even on the most tentative basis. There was something here that I did not understand. I knew only that I was before a wholly incomprehensible phenomenon.

What I had no doubt of was the scrupulous character of the testimonies I held. They were facts I could hold fast to. But two things came back into my mind again and again; the manner in which he had spoken of the ability and integrity of Major General Gubbins and the blaze of the eyes as he pronounced the word, 'Honest!' Those things did not go with the character of the man as indicated by the evidence. There was the mystery.

We went to the phone and Adam rang "Gilbert" and told him I had already made a *compte rendu* of the interview and asked him when he would like to see it. "Gilbert" said he would be free tomorrow morning.

'But I am not free tomorrow morning,' said Adam. 'Still, Miss Fuller is. I think you're both grown-up enough now to meet without me!'

It was arranged that "Gilbert" should come for me at my hotel at ten o'clock the next morning. I borrowed Adam's typewriter and spent the rest of the day tapping out my scribbles of the night, which I doubted if "Gilbert" would be able to read, and made at the same time a copy for him to keep if he liked.

Punctually at ten the next morning, he was at my hotel. I cast my eyes around seeking, perhaps rather too obviously, a secluded corner where we could settle.

'But we have nothing secret to talk about!' said "Gilbert", and found us a table near the window. I showed him my typescript and he read it through; he did not challenge the accuracy of the reporting but asked for some modifications, particularly that some of his own utterances should be taken out of quotation marks and paraphrased, where in their pristine form they were too vivid.

'For me it is not excluded that you were a German agent, purely and simply, from the time you first knew Boemelburg before the war, and that you were sent to England in 1942 by Boemelburg,' I cut in.

'You are wrong. I was in espionage before the war, but I have never been a German agent.'

'We won't go into that again. What I mean to say is that considering all the ambiguities that surround your history, I am being extremely decent with you.'

'Yes,' he said, 'but I am with you, too.'

We returned to the typescript and worked over some of the questions and answers together.

'You realise,' he said, 'that people are going to recognise me from this, even though you only say "Gilbert." All the people who *know* will know it's me and I don't want to look like a fool.'

The pseudonym, he pointed out, would only protect him from the curiosity of the grocer, the baker and the people with whom he worked, who knew nothing of these affairs. 'All the same,' he said, 'I'm sure I shall have telephone calls when this comes out.'

He was not very happy about it being said that his trial had been 'rigged.' I asked him why he had given June 2nd as the date of what used to be called his arrest. He did not know why it had been made June 2nd, he said. It was not he who had constructed the statement which he had made in court. It was 'they' who had suggested to him the lines which he had simply to follow, utilising certain elements which were true in a sense. That is to say, during the preliminary examination the *Juge d'Instruction* read him (as he was bound to) the text of an official statement received from London mentioning June 2nd and so on, and asked him if was true. Naturally he said, 'Yes.' What else could he have done in his position? It was this construction which he had later repeated when he went into the box.

'Who are *they*?' I asked. 'The people who arranged this construction?'

He could not give me the names. It would not be permissible. But he repeated that it all came from London. He agreed with me that it was 'they' also who had paid his fine and the costs of his defence at Croydon.

I told him I would have to put this in the book because it was important. He laughed and said, 'If you put that in the book I'll have trouble!'

I explained why I insisted in putting this in. 'I have always known there was something wrong in London, without knowing exactly what it was. The proof that there is something wrong is that they are susceptible to blackmail. And the proof that they are susceptible to blackmail is that they protected you. I don't want to do you any more harm than I can help, but you are the only instrument I can use.' (I was afterwards a little sorry for this choice of words, but at the time I was steeling myself to be hard).

'You have too much imagination. Blackmail is an awful word. You are crediting me with much more power than I have ever had. In any secret service the man who talks too much is disliked. The one who knows how to keep his mouth closed is appreciated. Not to speak of things I know does not mean blackmail. If I had blackmailed somebody I should be either very rich or very dead. And I am rich of a quiet life.'

He had simply let them know that he found himself in an embarrassing situation and asked if they would do something to get him out of it. They had responded in the manner he had told me.

This did not mean that he could not have obtained an acquittal otherwise.

Despite some insistence from me, he remained adamant that it was impossible to disclose the names. But he gave me to understand that it did not come from the "French Section", but from 'higher up.'

Returning voluntarily to the subject of Starr, he said, reflectively as though following on from a train of thought of his own, 'It's true, in one sense, that Starr and I are in opposition. But there is also a parallel.'

'Starr never worked for the Germans.'

'I am not making war on Starr. Don't think that. But the two cases, his and mine, are interesting to study together.'

I agreed with that. 'They are two faces of one coin.'

We were not thinking along quite the same lines, for his next remark was, 'They didn't charge Starr.'

'They smeared him!'

'But they didn't charge him. And they didn't charge me. They didn't charge anyone, in London.'

I saw the point he was making, but insisted on my own. 'They covered up for you and smeared him. At the time when I wrote *The Starr Affair* I had the feeling that he was being used as a scapegoat, but I thought it was for the mistakes of the Section in general; now I wonder whether it wasn't for you.'

He thought the search for scapegoats had been pretty general; nobody wanted to find himself the one left to carry the blame not only for his own faults but for everyone else's, too. Everyone knew things had gone wrong. Almost everyone had something to feel uneasy about and was anxious lest he be charged with complicity in more than was really his fault; if others shifted things on to him, in a situation where so many people had things to get themselves out of. He had already allowed that there was an opposition between his position and Starr's; but he wanted to make his point that in London they must have known that there was fault somewhere, yet they had charged no one and instituted no enquiry. That suggested something deep was involved.

There, for once, we were agreed.

When first he was sent into the field, he said, he thought it quite terrifying, having been in espionage before the war, to find himself operating with people who had no experience of secret work; and he was quite terrified, as well, to realise the extent of the penetration which, as was obvious to his perception, the Germans had already achieved. He couldn't go on in that without getting his own position put on a different basis. When he realised what a mess it all was, he thought the best job he could do was to get as many people as possible out by the aircraft he dispatched to England. That way he at least saved a certain number of lives.

I said I fully appreciated that he had got a very large number of people out of France in safety, some of whom felt they owed their lives to him since they were being hunted by the Gestapo. Perhaps he had been able to secure the immunity of

the departing aircraft only by his agreement with the Germans.
'But you paid it with the mail, and through that others lost
their lives.'

He would not have that.

It was utterly impossible, he maintained, to tell the whole
truth in these affairs. 'I don't care a fig for the truth — literal,
verbal truth — and I don't mind if you quote me for that!' He
was interested in archaeology and liked historical enigmas, but
this wasn't history yet.

He told me now that there had been a prior British
intervention on his behalf, in the early stages of the preliminary
examination. This was by an officer sent from London. I asked
him the name but he would not tell me, except that it was not
Boddington. 'Another.'

I had not told him that I already knew from Christmann,
who had been told by the Commissaire of the D.S.T. in 1946,
that there had in fact been an earlier British intervention. So
here, for the first time, I had the knowledge to check a
statement made in these matters by "Gilbert" and the check
proved positive. Excepting that at the time when Christmann
was told of the first British intervention "Gilbert" had not
been formally charged. It was, however, no secret that
unofficial investigations had begun before then. If Christmann
had not in fact been referring to the same intervention as
"Gilbert" was, then perhaps there was more than one. Madame
Guépin had spoken of an intervention from the British
Embassy, which did not sound much like "Gilbert's" officer
from London. It was hopeless to draw him further on this; he
was always closer with regard to those concerned with his case
in London than anything else.

Coming back to "Prosper" and "Archambault", he said
presently, 'Even if I had passed over the mail — which I don't

admit — it wouldn't have made any difference. They would have been arrested anyway, in a few days or a few weeks. It was only a question of time. The network had been penetrated already from so many sides it was bound to happen. The Germans did not need my services.'

I had to admit that that was probably true, though it didn't alter the position. 'According to Ernest it was, in fact, through the mail that it happened.'

'It could be, but anyway it was not me who gave it.'

He had he said had the choice of being tried by jury or before a panel of officers expert in these matters, and had chosen the latter, whose judgment was absolute. 'If they had found me guilty it would have been death, because there is no appeal against their verdict. You are not allowed to appeal, you have to accept it. But since they acquitted me they can never come back on it under any circumstances.' He had not wanted to live his life out under the fear that the charge might be reopened and so had staked everything upon the outcome, that day in the courtroom of the Reuilly Barracks. But now he was the gainer.

We had, by this time, got the waiter to bring us coffee and were much more relaxed. We talked now a little about his recent air smash, which had taken place in a fog. Immediately on crash-landing he had had, though slightly injured, to beat out the first flames with his bare hands in order to prevent the fire from spreading to the 8,000 litres (a little under 2,000 gallons) of fuel still in the tanks. The firemen were on the scene very quickly, but in the meantime he had coped with the worst danger. His hands had been burned; he showed them to me.

We also talked a little about my first two books, and he picked me up on a question concerning Muslim names in the first chapter of *Madeleine*. There was in fact an error in the French translation in which he had read it (though he read English without difficulty), which I had not had the opportunity to check, and so he was right on this point. From that, we passed to speaking of the Sufi school of mysticism in which Noor Inayat Khan, to give "Madeleine" her real name, had been brought up, and so to the religion of Islam. "Gilbert" said he believed he was the only Frenchman ever to have been within the sacred city of Mecca, a privilege not normally granted excepting to those of the Faith. 'I have ideas about religion,' he said.

'You have a religion?'

'Yes.'

'May I ask what it is?'

'Christian Science,' he said almost shyly.

This revelation made possible a deepening meeting-point. If Christian Science did not represent exactly my own line of thought, which was more Theosophic, yet it gave me more in common with him than if he had been a cynic. We found suddenly that we had a terrain upon which we could talk, if not quite in the same language, at least in language which held kindred ideas. I asked him in what way he understood some of the points special to Christian Science doctrine, and was amazed at the insight he showed in his replies. 'Believe me, I see clear,' he said.

At that moment, I had no doubt that he did.

In a lighter vein, he told me a personal story. When he was seventeen, he had a little gipsy girl-friend of about the same age. She introduced him to her mother, and her mother asked to be allowed to read his hand. He gave it to her; she studied it for a moment and reacted with more force than consideration for his feelings: he would die when he was thirty, she declared, or at least that would be for the best.

It gave him a bit of a turn, but he did not let it worry him too much. 'When one is seventeen, thirty seems quite old.' She had left him a reasonable span of years ahead, and he forgot about it.

His birthday was September 2nd, and September 2nd, 1939, was the eve of the war and saw the mobilisation of the French armed forces. Whilst the actual declaration of war did not come until the morrow, its imminence was already palpable; it was his thirtieth birthday, and whilst it was impossible reasonably to connect this forming up of the powers for battle with himself and the prophecy, yet the timing affected him. Almost in spite of himself, he felt that this day, or this birthday, should be his last. He thought he might be shot down whilst flying, or killed by a bomb. He tried to put the thought from him, and went out.

The first thing that happened was that he was caught in a motor accident in which he was nearly killed. A big lorry completely destroyed his small car. He escaped with incredible luck, and it left him feeling rather shaken. Later, while he was having dinner in a restaurant, a party of people who were nothing to do with him were having words; suddenly one of them, apparently quite drunk, pulled out a revolver and let it off. The bullet went through "Gilbert's" hair and into the wall behind. He remembered again that it was his thirtieth birthday, and went to bed carefully.

The next morning he said to himself that he was in his thirty-first year: he had perhaps outlived the fate that had been 'meant' for him; and he wondered what lay ahead.

On top of this story, I hesitated to suggest that he should show his palm to me; but I told him I had done a good deal of research into astrology, and he gave me at once complete data from which to erect a horoscope. On the spot, for I had an ephemeris for 1909, I drew him out a rough chart freehand and told him what seemed to me the most significant features. The horoscope was under the dominance of an almost exactly rising Neptune, and I explained to him all that implied in taste for adventure, on all planes and in all senses, embracing on the one hand that aspiration towards a mystical interpretation of the universe he had already declared, or an interest in the mysterious sides of mind and life, and on the other hand, on the mundane level, a penchant towards secret activities, with the liability to duplicity proceeding from such involvement. It was here that his drama lay; especially as the planet was caught up in a spectacular grand-cross which suggested a working out in violent terms. "Gilbert" was quite fascinated; and although he had never seen a chart before and the terms were strange to him, his acquaintance with Greek and Egyptian mythology enabled him, as I proceeded in my exposition, to pick up overtones of meaning I had thought it would be difficult to explain. His interest was intelligent and I promised (and later kept the promise) that after I returned to England I would send him a detailed and more fully considered delineation.

Before we parted, he produced from his pocket a *compte rendu* of the first interview which he himself had written out. There were seventeen pages of it on foolscap in his own hand. He had made it for himself, he said, as a memorandum, but it was of no use to him and I could have it. He wrote his real name on it, which I felt as a mark of confidence, and his address.

I promised to keep him informed of developments regarding the book and to give him warning before it appeared. 'Since I am dealing you a blow, I will let you know when it is going to fall.'

He seemed to have become quite reconciled now to the idea of publication; though a little anxious at moments, I could almost say that he seemed quite happy. 'It will cause me trouble,' he said, 'but that does not matter.'

CHAPTER TWELVE: REFLECTIONS

I had lunch with Yeo-Thomas and Barbara before leaving Paris and told them I had confronted "Gilbert" with the evidence I held against him and of the position which had been reached.

'He has really taken it rather well,' said Barbara.

That was my feeling, too; it really was worthy of note that he had at no time, even under hard attack, addressed an unpleasant word to me.

I showed Yeo-Thomas the agreed *compte rendu* of the conversations which had taken place between us, and he passed over the pages to Barbara as he finished reading them. When he came to the passages dealing with the manner in which the trial had been 'rigged', bearing upon the margins and back of the typescript some explanatory notes in "Gilbert's" hand, he could hardly believe his eyes. His first reaction was that if this appeared, "Gilbert" could probably still be charged with perjury; he was also shaken by the extent of the British involvement revealed. He was angry: 'This is the man who betrayed the whole "Prosper" network and left Norman's son to take the blame because he was dead.'

It was I who had collected the evidence; but I had sat beside "Gilbert" for many hours and, if he had not admitted fundamental guilt, he had owned up to things I never could have proven. That he had told me so much, knowing that I would expose his activities in the light in which I saw them, showed that he had nevertheless a trust in me that I would not use the matter in a malicious manner. Inasmuch as a confidence had thereby been placed in me, I felt I could not let it down. Adam had assured me that the authorities would not be able to come back on "Gilbert" even in respect of perjury; but I was, for all that, privately a little worried lest as the result of what "Gilbert" had authorised me to publish he might suffer adverse repercussions for which I should be responsible.

Yeo-Thomas said the French authorities were obviously not going to like it; they had been tricked, and could hardly be expected to take it kindly. It didn't do much of a job for Anglo-French relations either.

As he knew personally some of the French officials who would be most concerned, I asked him if he could not break the matter to them a little before the book appeared, if I could obtain "Gilbert's" permission for his intercession, and so take the edge off the shock of public revelation; if he could by explaining what had now happened take some of the sting out of it, they might not be vindictive.

Yeo-Thomas is most widely known for the heroism with which he served during the war and for his outspokenness; certainly he is a forthright man. But what never ceased to amaze me, and at times almost to take my breath, was the breadth of the charity and understanding to which he could rise at crises calling for qualities of a different order. I shall not forget the moments during which he wrestled with his anger and finally overmastered it. It was with a really sweet and kind smile that he said at last, 'I'll have a talk with them, if he is willing that I should.'

I felt it was almost superhuman.

Soon after my return to London I had dinner with Dame Irene Ward at the House and showed her, too, the papers I had brought back from Paris. There was so much to assimilate and so many issues to consider that we spent a whole series of evenings in conversation; I was never more grateful for her sympathy, support and balanced judgment. As always she did some probing on her own account. She was inclined to credit "Gilbert's" claim that he had, in fact, been authorised from one of the departments in London to make contact with the Germans in the capacity of double-agent, even if he sacrificed to the role more than was expected; otherwise, the repeated British interventions on his behalf would be inexplicable. If we had, in fact, been responsible, we could not have let him down when he was charged by the authorities of his own country; at the same time we would not have wanted to reveal the nature of our responsibility and so would have been in something of a fix.

It might be that S.O.E. and the services concerned with Intelligence were not so completely separated as was generally believed; there could be wheels within wheels, and perhaps a semi-secret service — secret at the time from the public at home but not alas from the enemy — was 'penetrated' in the interest of intelligence by a service more truly secret, 'Pukkah Secret Service!' She was also inclined to believe that a good many anomalies derived from the right hand not telling the left hand what it was doing, and vice versa; apart from the rivalries between the different organisations within S.O.E. and acting in liaison with it in respect of operations on the continent, there was the difference of attitude between the amateurs and the regulars; not only the agents sent out by S.O.E. but those at home who sent them out were mostly amateurs in secret work, and their activities were regarded with misgivings by those who had spent their lives in it. For herself, she believed there had been complications emanating from Vichy France and that political manoeuvres had, from first to last, played a role that had not yet been exposed and which exercised a disconcerting effect upon the conduct of operations. "Gilbert" was only part of a very much larger situation; it looked as though he might have been put into S.O.E. by Intelligence proper.

Unless he felt that he had some real basis from which his position could be defended, it seemed to her as it did to me inconceivable that he should have come forward to the extent that he had, and left in my hands the written evidence of our conversations.

'This country must have owed him something. That stands out a mile,' was her conclusion.

I had kept both Ernest and Christmann abreast of developments; and from both of them I received very nice letters expressing relief that the conversations with "Gilbert" had resulted in an accord. I fancied they had been a little anxious as to whether I should encounter a vicious reaction. It was strange how sympathies traversed frontiers.

From "Gilbert" himself I received within the month a long letter, seven pages on the same foolscap paper, handwritten and signed with his real name. There was nothing new in it; but I was glad to have it for it was friendly in tone and showed no desire to retract, as there might have been on reflection, his permission to publish as part of the book the agreed account of our conversations. There were patches of soreness, but the fairly steadily maintained tenor was that of reconciliation to the turn things were taking. On the human plane, the sky seemed to be lightening all round.

He asked me in his letter to remain impartial, and impartially I set before myself the issues. On the one hand, there was no proof that he had, in fact, been authorised during his visit to London in 1943 to continue the contact he had made with the Germans; on the other hand, had his association with the enemy been wholly unauthorised it seemed difficult to believe he would have been willing, even after his acquittal, to discuss it. Perhaps curiosity to know the evidence I held against him had prompted him in the first place to come and hear it; he might have calculated that having heard he would be better placed to combat, or thought to turn me from the publication. Yet having come and having heard, he had accepted that the book would appear, with no more than a mildly plaintive regret that he would appear in it as the arch villain, and a half-wistful half humorous reproach for having picked him out for the role. Had his activity been wholly shameful, it seemed to me almost inconceivable that he could have endured to sit hour after hour talking about it. Unless he were completely callous, which I did not think, the pain would have been unbearable. To have sent other men to their deaths, deliberately, one by one, for money, would have required an exceptionally cold and almost bloodless nature; but he was a warm and vibrant creature, impulsive and intuitional, a knave in some senses but not a knave devoid of sensibility. I did not think he would have sent men to their deaths in cold blood. It was difficult for me to know whether I was too hard or too soft with him. There was a lot of the *gamin* in him, but *gamin* plus something indefinable. He was not a materialist, and his approach to some questions was that of a mystic. At one moment, when we were speaking of Christian Science, he had said, 'It is within oneself that one makes the confession, and if the confession is sincere the absolution is assured. But then one should try to make some reparation.' He had not spoken that with personal reference; but after what had gone before, everything had personal reference. What remained with me was his gradual relaxation into near tranquillity, and the manner in which our conversations had changed key.

To bring my mind back to the practical issue: I had no doubt that he had passed the "Prosper" mail to the Germans, and also the times of the Lysander arrivals and departures; yet the tendency of the German services to play a waiting or observers' game over long periods could have led him to gauge occasionally amiss the extent to which they would be content to exercise mere surveillance or *contrôle* in the French sense. He had at one moment made the point that the mass arrests in June 1943 represented a change of policy upon the German side which completely took him by surprise. Again he could have overrated the strength of the bargaining power his unique position gave him. He did according to Ernest obtain the guarantee of safe departure from his fields of all who reached them, and unless I gave credit to the depositions of Bony and Lafont, which I knew false in the case of Starr, I knew of no occasion excepting the last before "Gilbert's" own departure for London, when arriving agents were in fact arrested after being trailed from the field. Then, as Ernest had pointed out, it was because "Gilbert's" usefulness had so nearly come to an end that Kieffer overstepped the limits of the agreement which had existed between them.

Again, considering the submission of the mail, it was a matter of Ernest's deduction and appreciation that this had been responsible for the arrest of "Prosper", "Archambault" and "Denise" by his service; but then Ernest had been unaware of the intervention of Christmann and "Anton" at the Square Clignancourt and of the series of meetings between them and "Archambault" and "Denise" and their colleagues which followed. It seemed to me now that "Archambault" and "Denise" must have been kept under German surveillance in consequence of these contacts and that they could have been arrested at any time after, even if there had been no mail; and the address of "Prosper's" hotel in the rue Mazagran could not have been in the mail. Looked at in this perspective, the importance of the mail receded. As for the Andrès report, its subject matter — the damage done by an R.A.F. bombing of certain works — could have told the Germans nothing they did not know better themselves.

The concept of the double-agent is well enough known to readers of the literature of espionage; it is understood well enough that the authorised double-agent may be instructed or licenced by his own side to contact the enemy and play in semblance the part of a traitor, in order to gain knowledge of the enemy's work such as he could scarcely obtain unless he became a part of the enemy's working machine; but is it so often asked what price he has to pay? For the enemy whose workings he penetrates in this way will certainly require something from him. The object is, of course, to gain more for his own side than he is obliged to give away to the other; one writer on these subjects has likened the process to the children's game of 'swops,' but in 'swops' as in any other contest one risks being the loser. The authorised double-agent who pays in good faith too dearly is not, therefore, a traitor, though of course such a double-agent may always turn real traitor, and the dividing line might be hard to draw.

If "Gilbert" had in contacting the Germans acted entirely without authorisation, then the repeated British interventions on his behalf would be inexplicable except on the hypothesis of something very wrong indeed in London, and on such a scale as to stagger the imagination; if on the other hand, one once accepted the proposition that his contacts with the German services had, at any rate in part, been authorised by some British department (not S.O.E.), everything fell into place. One could only regret that those responsible had not felt it possible to explain to their French allies what had really occurred.

The French authorities charged with conducting these investigations felt, I knew, that they had received little co-operation from this side of the Channel, that information and witnesses had been withheld from them and impediments deliberately placed in the way of their gaining evidence, that we had seemed to wish to shield the guilty for reasons not disclosed to them and that the manner in which we met them had not been above-board. We had not taken them into our confidence; faced only with our moves, they had had to put what construction on them they could. Some of the interpretations I had heard voiced, not in anger but seriously, would shock those who value the repute abroad of our services.

So far as S.O.E. was concerned, perhaps it had been hoped, vainly, that the French would never find out the mistakes that had been made in London, and in that hope it had been sought to cover up. But the shifts, to which recourse had been taken, had damaged French confidence in our honesty.

For a long time it indeed looked to me as though something sinister might be involved; now it seemed to me that the truth probably lay in nothing graver than an attempt to conceal how far the Germans had gained control of the organisation based on London. Those in the field who felt that the betrayal came from London had some justification, for the radio messages they received from London put them on occasions into contact with agents of the *Abwehr* and *Sicherheitsdienst*, but London (S.O.E.) was already itself deceived by incoming messages from other transmitters which had come to be German-controlled. It was in this way that London innocently played the intermediary between networks already taken over by the Germans, and those until that moment free.

Seeing that from the moment "La Chatte" arrived in England in February 1942, London knew that her radio set had been under German control since her capture the previous November, it is surprising that the possibilities inherent in German ability to play-back the radio sets were not thenceforth taken more seriously. There are indications that in certain cases 'London' was aware that it was with the Germans that radio communication was being made; but it may be that in those cases nothing but the minimum was sacrificed in an attempt to deceive the deceiver. There remain outstanding the cases where London continued for many months to send out not only cargoes of arms but new agents in response to German messages; of which perhaps the worst example in France was that of the Canadian circuit in the North. The two Canadians were captured on June 21st, 1943, having been parachuted only on the 18th, before they had even reached the area where they were to work, and their organisation was operated on their behalf, in radio communication with London, for a full year before, in June 1944, London at last ceased to make deliveries to it.

It was not only the agents sent out from London who lost their lives through these operations. The patriotic French of the territory who offered their homes and their co-operation were drawn into the trap. Perhaps it was because of the French life which had been lost in this way that it was felt particularly difficult after the war to explain to the French what had gone wrong.

The prestige of the British services regularly concerned with Intelligence had suffered by contamination, since continental authorities could scarcely be expected to appreciate that S.O.E. was a temporary organisation, responsible to the Cabinet, not through the Foreign Office but through another temporary organisation, the Ministry of Economic Warfare. That is why, if questions about it are raised today, it is difficult to find anybody to 'hold the baby.' Not only abroad but at home, amongst the public whose astonished eyes were first opened to the radio-game by Colonel Giskes's book, *Operation North Pole*, failure to appreciate that S.O.E. was a temporary and amateur creation has reflected adversely upon the repute of the regulars. How they operate, and whether they succeed or fail, never becomes known; but the operations of S.O.E. suddenly became public property after the war, because certain of those who served with the "French Section" wrote their stories or allowed them to be written, often in highly romancified and even fictionalised form, despite the claim to authenticity made in the preface or publisher's blurb. It may be felt they were less to blame for the mistakes they made during the war, since to make mistakes is human, than for the extent to which they subsequently thrust their personalities on the public, capitalising their participation and surrounding themselves with an aura they knew to be specious.

It is well known that S.O.E. was mainly an amateurs' organisation. But was it right that an organisation of this kind should be given into the hands of amateurs? The weakness of the amateur is often that he tends to be deceived in the beginning by beginner's luck, and so to underestimate the real complexity and difficulty of the work to which he has set his hand; as in most occupations, even the most capable need time to gain experience, and in this operation that time cost lives. Who except amateurs could have thought it suitable or right to send into the field some of the very young and inexperienced people whom they did?

What qualifications other than idealism and bravery had young girls like "Denise" and "Madeleine" to pick their way in that complex underworld into which they were dropped? On first reading Placke's deposition concerning the meeting at the Café Colisée, I remembered with a shudder the young girl, even less worldly experienced than I was at the same age, who perched on the side of my divan reading lines from the *Bhagavad Gita*. She had lived at home with her mother until the war, played the harp, written fairy stories for children, and studied the mystical books of the East among which she had been brought up. What hope had a girl like that when put, by chiefs in London already themselves deceived, into contact with a German agent of the experience of Placke?

What had "Archambault," poor Norman's son, younger even than "Madeleine," yet "Prosper's" second-in-command, done before the war? He had been apprenticed in a very respectable firm of chartered accountants. Could he really be expected, with that background, to be a match for operators as subtle as Christmann and "Anton," with whom he too was put into contact by London through the radio-game?

Before they left England, agents were given intensive physical training, but it was not only bodily fitness that they required in the field; and the kind of knowledge they needed for their security was not the kind that could be taught during a few weeks' security course at a school in the New Forest. How can people be taught how to recognise when those with whom they have to deal are playing them false, or how to deal wisely with relations in which they suspect falsity? These are things that only years of living in the world can teach, and not always then.

The networks which survived were those in the wild mountainous areas, mostly in the South and the Midi. Encamped with the *Maquis* on densely wooded slopes, the agents sent to these regions lived a rough life, but, having little contact except with the limited community of the local people, they were less liable to German penetration than in urban areas with a shifting population. It was in the towns and cities where they had to meet in cafés or keep appointments with personally unknown 'contacts' who would identify themselves by the pronunciation of some set phrase acting as password, that the rot set in.

Here it was not only human maturity but knowledge of the gambits possible in a very particular kind of world that was required. It would, I think, not be wrong to say that most of our agents, when they were sent out, took it for granted that the aim of the Gestapo was to capture them as quickly as it could locate them. They were taught in England how to notice if they were being shadowed and how to elude a shadow. So long as they were not captured they imagined they were not caught. How were they to learn until it was too late, that agents of the *Sicherheitsdienst* or *Abwehr* would take an aperitif with them in a café and let them go their ways, after making an arrangement to meet again? Or enact charades, arresting each other before them that they might report what they had seen to London? The Germans made circles round them. It was not, of course, intended that the young people sent out by S.O.E. "French Section", who were expected to work very much in their own group, should find themselves in contact with agents of the German counter-espionage or with double-agents; but that those in London who sent them out did not foresee that they would, in fact, be exposed to such contacts, showed that they did not themselves understand the world into which they plunged them. S.O.E. was an amateurs' organisation. If operations of this sort have to be launched, perhaps it would be better that they should be conducted by those experienced in secret work.

Between people who have lived in the same kind of *ambiance*, there may be some kind of understanding of each other's way of thinking. But the mixture of professionals with amateurs (in the way Dame Irene used the terms) made that almost impossible and gave rise to something near antipathy.

The special difficulty of "Gilbert's" position lay in that, unlike the ardent and inexperienced young people generally recruited by S.O.E., he had been in secret work before the war, and so had quite a different approach to some questions. It had been decided for certain reasons that he should work in the field through S.O.E., but once there, he felt, in the "French Section" networks, like a fish out of water. Appreciating the extent of what he succinctly described as 'the mess,' he had attempted to pull some of the chestnuts out of the fire in his own way. It was difficult to see what else he could have been expected to do.

I had followed the track of "Gilbert," but what in fact did it lead to? Whatever the nature of his own involvement, whether he was a traitor or whether his contacts with the Germans were authorised, whether he should have been found guilty had the whole truth been available to the court which tried him, or whether the verdict arrived at was in fact the right one, even though the defence had been organised upon a false basis, his case had clearly been a source of embarrassment to the British. Enquiry into these operations had never been encouraged in London. At first I had thought it was on account of the deception S.O.E. had suffered through the radio-game, later it became apparent that something more was involved. Now it seemed that the case of "Gilbert" was that something more. Perhaps there were other things as well; indeed I had come across other trails. But without looking for anything more sinister, I felt that I had at last discovered a sufficient reason for the sensitivity so marked in certain quarters.

I saw now a situation where so many had tried as best they knew, where so many had made mistakes or been at fault, where so many had died in consequence of those mistakes and faults, where so many had distorted truth to protect themselves and others, that it seemed no longer availing to seek out any one as an especial target for blame. The responsibility had been, and should in fairness be allowed to remain, a distributed one.

I had been upturning stones now for more than eight years. If under some of them I had found strange creeping things of unattractive character, I had also found goodness, charity, moral courage and trust, and sometimes I had found those things where they might not have been expected. Whilst writing these reflections four lines of doggerel verse kept running in my mind:

> There is so much good in the worst of us,
> And so much bad in the best of us,
> That it ill behoves any one of us
> To judge another of us.

If the second line is salutary to remember, to the first I can bear witness. It is the lasting thought I should like to leave with the reader. For therein lies the capacity of the human heart to gain the day.

EPILOGUE: "GILBERT" READS THE MSS.

Throughout the summer, "Gilbert" continued to maintain contact with me by letter with a steadiness which increased my respect. When the manuscript was completed — all but this last — I wrote that I would be willing for him to see it in its entirety and, since it was he who bore the brunt of the charges, to let him have the last word. If he would like to write a paragraph or so of his own which I could put at the end of the book, I would gladly include it. He replied by return saying he would accept this invitation and enclosing, in English, a handwritten statement signed with his real name and very generously worded: but worded as though he had read and approved the whole manuscript already. For somebody who had lived through so much duplicity, he was certainly very trusting; the manuscript might have contained even worse against him than I had given him to understand. Whilst very much touched by this faith, I preferred he should know what he was signing for. Accordingly, I brought the manuscript with me to Paris in the last week of August, 1957. "Gilbert" was at Orly to meet me as I came off the plane; and I stepped into his car to be driven into Paris by my victim.

He asked almost immediately if the little piece he had written was all right.

'It's very generous; but you wrote it without knowing what you were letting yourself in for.'

'I thought it would help the book. I thought it would add authenticity if I said I had read it.' This reply, almost incredible in the circumstances, I found again very touching. Perhaps I should say, in so many words, that he never asked for a cut, and had no financial interest to allow the publication to proceed.

As he was driving, "Gilbert" explained to me that the violence of his first reaction to a scandal involving his name had been partly because the prospect had burst upon him at a moment that seemed crucial in his career. Following the dreadful air crash, he had thought he might have to give evidence if there was an enquiry, and his first thought had been that he needed to keep his mind clear for that, and not encumbered with other problems deriving from the past. The crash in itself was hard enough, and he had felt it was not the time to have the old spying business dragged out. Indeed, it had appeared to him that there could not be a worse moment for having his war record again called into question. However, things had not worked out badly. The enquiry had turned well for him. He was back on flying again, and did not feel now that it mattered so much.

He felt the publication was bound to cause him some embarrassment, but he thought he could stand up to it. He did not propose to alter the routine of his life in any way. When the book came out, he would carry on as usual; and if there were any *ennuis*, he would cope with them as they came.

That "Gilbert" had physical courage had never been in question; I felt now that the resolution to which he had come showed a good deal of moral courage also.

He set me down at my hotel in Montmartre, to return later in the day for work.

"Gilbert" read the whole manuscript, seated at my side, from the first page to the last. The sessions took place in a spirit of complete good will. The last occupied fourteen hours, broken only for meals which we took together; he came at nine in the morning and stayed until eleven in the evening when we finished it. There had been a whole evolution since our first encounter in May and, if I did not at all moments believe his words, and if he understood that and did not bear me malice on account of it, a confidence had nevertheless been established. I knew that he felt the reading of the manuscript as an ordeal but, if it was in places hard for him, it did not diminish his friendliness. Apart from a rather wistful complaint, when he had got through about half of it, that he appeared as 'black, black,' he made no reproaches. Much of the text, especially where it concerned himself, he murmured half aloud, sometimes stopping to put his finger on a line and debate its significance. He gave me his running commentary as he went along, sometimes piquant or amusing, sometimes charged with a good deal of emotion, but never with hostility towards myself.

I had brought with me, to show him, photostatted copies which I had had made of the six sheets of Ernest's testimony concerning him, so that he could study it in the original handwriting and in the original language, French. I tried to give them into his hand, but he pushed them back to me gently, saying he was sure I had reproduced them honestly in the manuscript and that he would trust my translation into English.

He read Ernest's statement, in my text, attentively but without comment, and passed straight on.

When we came to the French newspaper reports of his trial, he smiled a little at the reporters' having given him credit for his 'good taste' in removing from his buttonhole the ribbon of the Légion d'Honneur and other decorations. It was not, he said, left to the discretion of the accused. 'They take your decorations off you just before you go into the courtroom, and afterwards they give them back to you as you leave. If you have been acquitted, of course. *C'est tout de même impressionant.'*

I asked him not to mark the manuscript, so he collected his serious points on a separate sheet.

1. Chapter 4. With regard to my question whether Boddington had received official authorisation from London to give evidence at his trial, he affirmed that that was so.

2. Same Chapter, Ernest's letter to me, on p. 75. He would like to underline the sentence: *'Kieffer knew that he [Boddington] was coming some days before his arrival in Paris.'* This line did not otherwise draw attention to itself. Perhaps it had little importance to Ernest, but it had a great deal to him.

3. Just below, p. 76, where Ernest quoted Agazarian, he was angered by the word 'fled.' He wanted to add a footnote and to sign it: *'Boddington did not fly. Gilbert.'* Boddington, he said, went back to England quietly, in his own time.

4. Chapter 7. With regard to my speculations on p. 118-9, he had at the time in question been ignorant of Operation North Pole.

5. Chapter 9, the confusion at the Square Clignancourt. He never received instructions from London to meet any agent coming from Holland. The first he heard of it was from Agazarian. It was not "Archambault" but Agazarian who lived only a few doors from himself, who came to tell him that an agent from Holland was looking for him and had gone to the Square Clignancourt, where he seemed to expect to find him, but where he met "Archambault" instead, apparently as the result of some confusion. Agazarian told

"Gilbert" that a further meeting between the Dutchman "Anton" and members of the "Prosper" network had been arranged to take place at the Restaurant Capucines, and he suggested to "Gilbert" that he should come along to the Capucines as the easiest place at which to meet "Anton." As "Gilbert" had received no instructions from London to meet anybody coming from Holland and did not wish to meet somebody whose role he did not understand, he thought it wiser not to go. Agazarian did go, and afterwards came back in a state of great distress to tell him that whilst they were all there the Germans had entered and arrested "Anton," and that the rest of them had only escaped by the skin of their teeth. "Gilbert" felt sure that Agazarian did not suspect that "Anton" was himself a German; neither, he affirmed, did he know it. In parenthesis, he had not realised that there were two agents from Holland; until his conversations with me he had been under the impression that "Anton" and Christmann were two names for one person.

6. Despite the witness of Madame Fèvre that "Prosper" had been arrested at the hotel in the rue Mazagran between 10 and 11 on the morning of June 24th (and that the Germans had been waiting there for him since 1 a.m.), he maintained that he had learned of it at 9 a.m. from "Antoine" near the Gare St. Lazare. It was, he suggested, possible that "Prosper" had been conducted back to his hotel afterwards under escort, as "Denise" had been taken back to her lodgings at 51 rue des Petites Ecuries, with "Archambault", although they had been arrested together at his place in the

small hours of the same morning. Whatever the explanation, he affirmed that he himself had had an appointment to meet "Prosper" with "Antoine" at a café opposite the Hotel Terminus close to the Gare St. Lazare at 9 on the morning in question. As was his custom when keeping a rendezvous, he went an hour early and surveyed the place agreed upon from the pavement opposite, standing by the terrace of the Terminus. Then he walked around, bought newspapers and so on to fill up the hour and at 9 o'clock he saw "Antoine" approach from the southwest pavement of the rue de Rome, cross the road and enter the café. He waited five minutes more, then entered the café himself; the first words "Antoine" spoke to him were, '"Prosper" has been arrested.' It had happened, "Antoine" told him, under his very eyes and only a moment previously. At this distance of time, "Gilbert" could not be sure whether "Antoine" said it had happened in the station as "Prosper" was getting out of the train or 'in the first café where he was due to meet "Antoine" before meeting me' — presumably the latter. It was, he pointed out, not to his interest to disclose that he had been a party to this rendezvous (a fact I had not known until he told me), since anybody who had knowledge of it might be suspected as a possible source of leakage. The Mazagran story would appear to let him out altogether and it might therefore seem to his advantage to leave well alone. If he insisted on this episode by the Gare St. Lazare, it was because really it had occurred as he said.[62]

____

[62] Some of "Gilbert's" points concerning the St. Lazare episode,

After he had finished reading the whole, I showed him the paragraph he had written for me to put at the end, and gave him the opportunity to make any modifications he wished now that he had studied the manuscript. As his command of English syntax was uncertain, and he had here and there used a word inappropriate to express his meaning as he explained it to me in French, I asked him if he would like me to straighten out the passage. To this he readily agreed, saying he would prefer it to read in correct English. I had slightly to recast some of the phrases, and we were now working against time, for he had to be at the airport in order to fly an aircraft due to take off at midnight on a long-distance flight; nevertheless he understood and approved what I did in reshaping the syntax and the words which appear as an epilogue are still substantially his own.

This might have been the last I heard of "Gilbert," since he could at this point have washed his hands of the affair completely. Nevertheless, he maintained touch by letter. Not long after our reading of the manuscript he had another accident, this time by water. Crossing a river, somewhere in the Far East, in a boat which capsized amidst rapids, and, though able to swim like a seal, he was dashed with violence against the rocks. The 'wounds,' he wrote, presumably cuts, were in

---

though included here for convenience, he in fact sent me subsequently in a letter together with a sketch map and an extract from a deposition made on 4/7/47 by Madame Guepin saying that on the 22nd June she lunched in Paris with "Prosper", "Archambault" and "Denise" when they discussed an expected parachute delivery, that on the 23rd "Prosper" had come to Gisors where he spent the night at her house, and that when he left the next morning at 7 o'clock he told her he had an appointment in Paris at 9, though she did not know where or with whom. It was the last line which interested "Gilbert" as affording independent support for his affirmation that "Prosper" had an appointment for 9 a.m.

themselves minor, but due to the absence of medical supplies or a doctor took on a more serious character; when eventually he reached hospital he had high fever, and had to be kept for some time in bed. Now he had returned to flying.

The above was already in print when "Gilbert" sent me, still from the Far East, copied extracts from two depositions concerning BOE 48 and the meeting in the empty apartment apparently made by Ernest early in 1947. The point made by "Gilbert" was that these, having been in French possession, must have been taken into consideration prior to his acquittal. I supposed it might have been considered improper, especially since the accused was standing trial on a capital charge, to admit as evidence for the prosecution written testimony from a witness who could not be put into the box to stand cross-examination by the defence. Nevertheless, I checked at once with Ernest by letter and he replied that he had, while at the American camp in Dachau, twice been visited by a French officer, about the time in question, and each time requested to make a statement concerning "Gilbert." He had kept no copy but there seemed no reason to doubt the authenticity of those "Gilbert" had sent me. Except that as in the 1949 deposition to the authorities in Paris, "Claude" was given as an additional alias of "Gilbert," the substance was identical with that which Ernest had communicated to me, though written so much closer to the events. My eye was caught, however, by the word "tall." I had not mentioned to "Gilbert" that Ernest had spoken the word "tall" to me (I only put it into the manuscript after this). I had discounted it as a subjective impression outweighed by Ernest's recognition of the photograph. As "Gilbert" still maintained that the man whom Goetz took Ernest to meet in the empty flat was not himself, I wrote to him that there would be only one way to settle this question:

by a confrontation. Would he be willing, on his return to Europe, to come with me to Germany and let me present him to Ernest and ask Ernest whether he recognised in him or not the man he had met with Goetz in that empty flat? "Gilbert" replied that he would be willing, adding helpfully that he did not think he had changed much in appearance since 1944.

"GILBERT'S" PARAGRAPH

I have read the whole script of Miss Jean Overton Fuller, and to the parts treating of events in which I was concerned I can put my signature. I lived them in the atmosphere described. Nevertheless, I do not agree with Ernest as regards the whole of his statement, or with Christmann on some small points; and I do not agree with Madame Aigrain. I can sleep at peace because I know that I was not responsible for the arrest of "Prosper," "Archambault," or any others. But seeing things now through the eyes of different people, and in a different perspective, I realise they can look different from what they were in truth.

I, like any other British, German or French agent, have to recognise that we could have been abused. We were blind fighting in darkness. To be successful in the missions for which we were responsible, we had often to clear from our way possible causes of nuisance. We used to risk our lives every day, three times a day, with no rest or encouragement. We were rich in what we had in our hearts and in our minds. Today I am rich in the friendship of the people who know what I did.

I can't and won't say more. I prefer to let Miss Jean Overton Fuller's book make its way on her own responsibility.

DATES FOR REFERENCE

1942

"Gilbert" arrives from France, serves with R.A.F. Special Squadron

July: "Jacqueline" landed in France by boat.

24th September: "Denise" and Lise de Baissac parachuted, received by Culioli.

1st (?) October: "Prosper" parachuted.

1st November: "Archambault" parachuted, received by Culioli.

1943

23rd January: "Gilbert" parachuted back to France on to a field near Pithiviers in the Loiret to take up duties as Air Movements Officer to S.O.E.

22nd April: Arrest of Tambour sisters.

Easter: "Gilbert" makes a brief visit to London; returns.

27th May: Christmann and "Anton" visit Square Clignancourt, and meet "Archambault" and "Denise," Marcel Charbonnier and Alain Bussoz.

2nd June: Same party reassembles, plus Agazarian, at Restaurant Capucines. Mock arrest of "Anton."

2nd June (also): Date cited by "Gilbert" in another context.

10th June: "Prosper" leaves for London, seen off by "Gilbert."

16th June: "Madeleine" landed by Lysander, received by "Gilbert."

18th June: The two Canadians parachuted.

20th June: "Prosper" returns from London, received by Culioli.

21st June: The two Canadians, Culioli and "Jacqueline" arrested.

24th June: "Prosper", "Archambault" and "Denise" arrested.

1st July: Lequeux arrested.

15th July: Boddington and Agazarian parachuted (latter after brief visit to London), received by "Gilbert."

18th July: Starr arrested.

15th or 16th August: Boddington returns to London together with "Antoine," Lise de Baissac and others, seen off by "Gilbert."

Late August: Meeting at the Café Colisée between "Madeleine" and Placke and Holdorf.

12th October: Madame Aigrain and Andrès arrested.

13th October: "Madeleine" arrested.

18th October: Garry and his wife arrested.

18th November: Starr's radio operator and courier arrested.

1944

4th February: "Gilbert" recalled to London for questioning.

29th February: "Antoine", Lionel Lee and Madeleine Damerment parachuted, met on field by *Sicherheitsdienst*.

1st September: "Gilbert" freed, on the completion of his questioning in London, to rejoin the Air Force.

9th September: "Gilbert" shot down.

10th September: Bony and Lafont's depositions.

1945

8th May: End of war with Germany.

18th October: Lequeux's trial at Orleans.

1946

1st April: Placke's deposition.

11th April: "Gilbert" apprehended at Croydon.

23rd April: "Gilbert's" trial at Croydon.

25th May: Ernest arrested by the Americans.
26th November: "Gilbert" arrested in Paris.

1947

1st April: Ernest fetched from the Americans by the British.
Mid July: French ask British for Ernest; Ernest sent back to
Americans.

1948

7th June: "Gilbert's" trial in Paris.
9th June: Culioli's first trial in Paris.

1949

17th March: Culioli's retrial at Metz.
End April: Ernest escorted to Paris for questioning by French
authorities.
June: Author began her researches.

1950

March: Ernest released with *Non Lieu*, returns to Germany.
17th-26th June: Author's first interviews with Ernest.
27th June: Starr receives *Non Lieu*.

1954

12th November: Ernest makes statement on "Gilbert" for
author.

1957

May: Author's first interviews with "Gilbert."

BIBLIOGRAPHY

(Works useful to consult in conjunction with the present)

London Calling North Pole by H. J. Giskes, Kimber, 1953.

Inside North Pole by Pieter Dourlein, Kimber, 1953.

The White Rabbit (story of Yeo-Thomas) by Bruce Marshall, Evans, 1952.

Madeleine by Jean Overton Fuller, Gollancz, 1952, out of print; revised edition under title *Born for Sacrifice*, Pan Books, 1957.

The Starr Affair by Jean Overton Fuller, Gollancz, 1954; Panther Books, 1957.

Colonel Henri's Story edited by Ian Colvin, Kimber, 1954.

F.A.N.Y. Invicta by Irene Ward, Hutchinson, 1955.

The Cat with Two Faces by Gordon Young, Putnam, 1957.

In French:

La Sologne au Temps de L'Héroisme et de la Trahison by Paul Guillaume, Imprimerie Nouvelle, 8 ter Faubourg Madeleine, Orléans, 1950.

In German:

La Chatte by Erich Borchers, Adolf Sponholtz Verlag, Hannover, 1950.

Monsieur Jean by Erich Borchers, Adolf Sponholtz Verlag, Hannover, 1951.

A NOTE TO THE READER

If you have enjoyed this book enough to leave a review on **Amazon** and **Goodreads**, then we would be truly grateful.

The Estate of Jean Overton Fuller

Sapere Books is an exciting new publisher of brilliant fiction and popular history.

To find out more about our latest releases and our monthly bargain books visit our website: **saperebooks.com**